W9-CAV-299

Countryside of China

Guo Huancheng, Ren Guozhu & Lü Mingwei

translation by Tong Xiaohua

CHINA
INTERCONTINENTAL
PRESS

JOURNEY INTO CHINA

Counsellor: Cai Wu
General Director: Li Bing
Chief Editors: Guo Changjian & Li Xiangping
Deputy Chief Editor: Wu Wei

图书在版编目（CIP）数据

乡村之旅：英文/郭焕成，任国柱，吕明伟著；童孝华译
—北京：五洲传播出版社，2007.8
（中国之旅）
ISBN 978-7-5085-1096-5

I．乡…
II．①郭… ②任… ③吕… ④童…
III．乡村－概况－中国－英文
IV．K928.5

中国版本图书馆CIP数据核字（2007）第064535号

COUNTRYSIDE OF CHINA

Author: Guo Huancheng, Ren Guozhu & Lü Mingwei
Translator: Tong Xiaohua
Planner: Feng Lingyu
Project Director: Deng Jinhui
Executive Editor: Gao Lei
Art Director: Tian Lin
Photo Credit: Imagine China, China Foto Press,
    China Intercontinental Press, Lü Mingwei
Publisher: China Intercontinental Press (6 Beixiaomachang, Lianhuachi
    Donglu, Haidian District, Beijing 100038, China)
Printer: Beijing Picture in Picture Printing Co., Ltd.
Tel: 86-10-58891281
Website: www.cicc.org.cn
Edition: Aug. 2007, 1st edition, 1st print run
Format: 787×1092mm 1/16
Signatures: 11
Words: 52,000
Print Run: 1–7,000
Price: RMB 98.00 (yuan)

Contents

Foreword 5

Traditional Homes with Picturesque Beauty 9
Shuhe, an Ancient Naxi Town in Lijiang 11
Houses on Stilts and the Wind-Rain Bridge: Dong Villages in
   Liping 15
Hakka Civilian Dwellings: Yongding Earthen Houses 19
Residence of a Shanxi Businessman: The Grand Courtyard of
   Qiao Family 24
Xidi and Hongcun: Ancient Villages in Huizhou 28
Cuandixia Village: Ancient Village in Western Beijing 33
Zhouzhuang: A Town of Rivers and Lakes in Southern China 38
The Immigrant Town of Nianbadu 43
Kaiping, Guangdong: East Meets West in the Diaolou 46
Jiaju Tibetan Village, the Most Beautiful Village in China 51

Rustic Scenes All over China 57
Wuyuan: Possibly the Most Beautiful Countryside 59
Shuangfeng Forestry Center: Snow Village in the Northeast 63
Tuva Village Beside Kanasi Lake 68
The Terraced Fields of the Hani People in Yuanyang 74
Puli Town, Nantou County 78
Fishing Tourism on Changdao Island 83
Turpan Grape Valley 88
Tengtou Village of Fenghua, Zhejiang 94
Guangxi Buluotuo Scenic Mango Orchard 99

The Rich Traditions of Folk Culture 103

Lugu Lake: Exotic Oriental Land of Women   105

Forced Marriage of the Yi Ethnic Group   111

Northern Shaanxi: Simple Yet Precise Village Marriage
Ceremony 116

Southern China: Dragon Boat Races on Duanwu   121

Shehuo of the Central Plains   125

Traditional Wooden Chinese New Year Pictures of
Yangjiabu, Weifang   130

Farmer Art Village in Jinshan District, Shanghai   135

Home of Plaster Statues—Liuying (Camp Six) Village in
Fengxiang, Shaanxi   139

The New Appearance of the New Countryside 143

Rural Tourism in Nongke Village in Pixian, Sichuan   145

Hancunhe, the Richest Village in Beijing's Suburbs   149

Home to Longjing Tea—Longjing Village   153

Model of Common Prosperity—Huaxi Village   157

Eco-Friendly Village: Liuminying   161

Xibaipo Red Tourism   165

Tahur Hala New Village   170

Foreword

The countryside usually refers to the large areas outside of the cities. It developed from the first humans living together and is the place where we have been living for generation after generation. In the early living and working activities of our ancestors, people lived together to pool their resources to better defend themselves, thrive and gather resources. This concentration of people living together represents the earliest stage in the formation of the countryside in China. The formation of the countryside followed a slow process that took a million years from the first concentration of dwellings to living in caves and living near vegetation and water to scattered settlements in the countryside (semi-permanent settlements) to fixed villages in the countryside to fixed settlements of permanent residents. During the process of moving from living in caves and outside to living in buildings, after the beginning of division of labor, society entered the stage of scattered village settlements. As the level of agricultural production went up, the scattered settlements went from scattered and semi-permanent to become more stable as the size and scope of settlements grew. The development of the countryside in China was a slow process of change that began with a primitive form of villages that developed into ancient style of villages and finally the modern form of villages. As of the 1990s there were approximately 3.207 million incorporated villages in China containing 205 million households inhabited by 790 million people. During the long process of change and development in the Chinese countryside, the hardworking, simple people of ancient China developed a brilliant farming culture and ethnic traditions, writing chapter after chapter in the history of the peoples in the world.

China has a vast territory and long history with great differences in natural conditions among different areas of the country. The natural resources and cultural content of the villages are very rich. The beautiful natural scenery of the Chinese countryside, the ancient village buildings, the authentic folk customs, the longstanding farming culture, the simple and unsophisticated village workshops and the primitive form of labor create a unique vista in the countryside. It is like a scene in a painting of the countryside reflecting perfect harmony between people and nature. For example, the row on row of the terraced fields in Yuanyang, Yunnan, forestry farms in the snowed-capped Changbai Mountains, a sea of flowers in Wuyuan in spring, Zhouzhuang, a town of rivers and lakes in southern China and the melons in Turpan, Xinjiang. There are also country villages and dwellings that combine the thousands of years of traditional Chinese culture with religious ideals and folk customs. Examples of such historical buildings include the dwellings of the Naxi people on the Shuhe in Lijiang, Yunnan, the stockaded villages of the Dong people of Liping, Guizhou, the earthen buildings of the Hakka people of Yongding, Fujian, The grand courtyard of Qiao Family in Shanxi, the Huizhou dwellings of Hongcun and Xidi villages in Anhui and the watchtowers of Kaiping, Guangdong that combine Chinese and Western influences. There are also rural festivals, farming techniques, lifestyles and interesting tales that are rich in cultural content such as the *Shehuo* of the Central Plains and the dragon boat races of southern China. Moreover, China has 56 officially recognized ethnic groups including the Dai people of Yunnan, the Miao people of Guizhou, the Zhuang people of Guangxi, the Yao people of Hunan, the Li people of Hainan, the Uygur people of Xinjiang and the Tibetan people of Tibet, all of whom attract people to enjoy their local customs. These ethnic minority groups are good at singing and dancing. They are ebullient and unrestrained and have maintained their unique lifestyles and customs for generation after generation in the areas they inhabit, providing ample resources for tourists.

The Chinese countryside has been undergoing great changes since the government began instituting the reform and opening up policy. The rural economy has been developing rapidly. The lives of rural residents have greatly improved. The appearance of the countryside has changed considerably. The Chinese government has recently introduced the goals and requirements for building a new socialist countryside. Rural dwellers across the country are developing modern agriculture, improving the rural living environment, and building a new socialist countryside. During this process, a great many model villages and model plots for modern agriculture such as Huaxi Village in Jiangsu, Hancunhe Town, and Liuminying eco-friendly farms in Beijing and Longjing Village in Hangzhou, Zhejiang. These model villages and agricultural plots are prime examples of the new image and appearance of the new socialist countryside.

Countryside of China shows the natural and social phenomena of these villages in the Chinese countryside through a combination of tradition and modernity. The book provides a detailed description of 30-plus selected villages in China using both text and illustrations. The book covers traditional dwellings, folk customs and marriage customs, farm life, country scenes, farming culture, ethnic culture and the building of a new socialist countryside, reflecting the unique traditions of various types of villages in different regions of the country. It could be said that *Countryside of China* is a tour to see the natural and human sights in the Chinese countryside, as well as a tour to see the folk customs and culture in the countryside and a tour to see ethnic minority culture. The abundant natural resources, agricultural resources, human resources, and folk culture resources are the outstanding features of the Chinese countryside. The countryside attracts large numbers of Chinese city dwellers, resulting in a great exchange of concepts, culture, news, and knowledge between urban and rural areas of the country. Moreover, the Chinese countryside is attractive to

overseas tourists who come to appreciate the folk customs of Chinese rural residents, thereby increasing understanding among different peoples of the world and promoting mutual development of all countries of the world.

Anything to do with national culture belongs to the world. The countryside of this rapidly developing country of China, with its unique mix of ethnic groups, is now coming into view for our friends at home and abroad and becoming a focal point for increasing friendship among the peoples of the world. The countryside of China is welcoming friends from all over the world with their new image and enthusiasm.

Guo Huancheng

March 6, 2007

Traditional Homes with Picturesque Beauty

During the many thousand years when people lived in an agricultural society, the level of productive forces was quite low. People took a simple ecological outlook and created the best possible living environment for themselves by conforming to nature and building a suitable living environment using simple techniques. Traditional Chinese homes were adapted to local natural conditions and climate and drew of the rich sensitivity and aesthetic sensibility of their builders. Because the natural conditions and cultural situation differed from place to place, a great diversity of house styles appeared that was rarely matched in the history of architecture.

Many traditional houses still exist in rural areas all around the country, and people still think of them as the ideal type of residence.

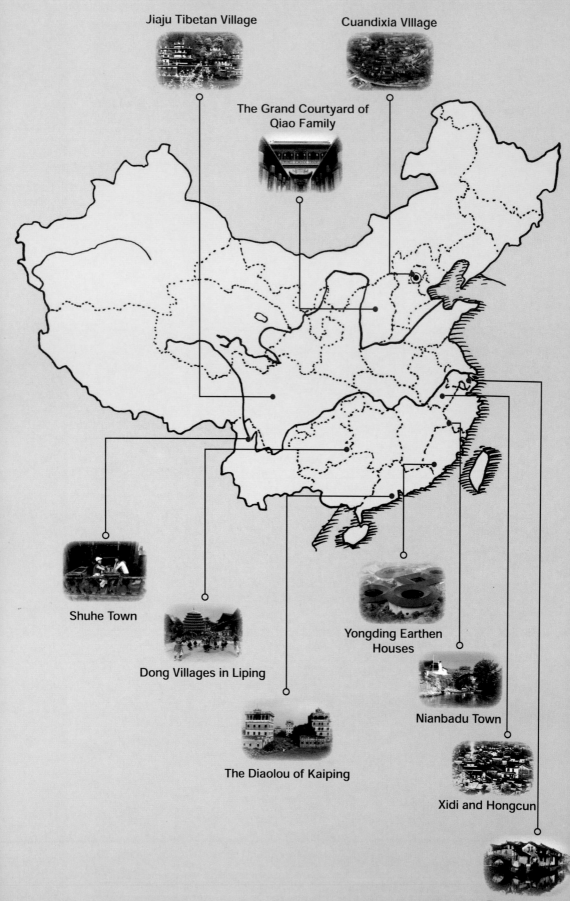

Jiaju Tibetan Village

Cuandixia VIllage

The Grand Courtyard of Qiao Family

Shuhe Town

Dong Villages in Liping

The Diaolou of Kaiping

Yongding Earthen Houses

Nianbadu Town

Xidi and Hongcun

Zhouzhuang

Shuhe, an Ancient Naxi Town in Lijiang

T he ancient town of Shuhe is located in Lijiang in the northwest part of Yunnan and was once an important town on the "ancient tea delivery road." Driving to Shuhe from Lijiang only requires following the pavement 7 kilometers towards Snow Mountain before the ancient village comes into view. This is Shuhe, the "land of clear springs," also known as Longquan (Dragon Springs) Village.

Shuhe is the location of one of the earliest settlements

Bird's-eye view of the ancient town in the first light of day

of Naxi people. Entering the ancient village you can directly arrive at the central square in the style of Sifang Street in the ancient city of Lijiang. The square has a total area of 200 square meters and has become known as "Shuhe's Sifang Street." The four sides of the square are lined with shops and stores with ancient-style wooden fronts painted with bright red lacquer. Added to the shiny black stones in front of the stores and the spotted stone walkways, the square has a simple and natural feel.

Elderly Naxi woman in a lane

West of Sifang Street at the foot of the mountains is a large concentration of ancient dwellings. Most of the Naxi dwellings in Shuhe are made of earth and wood, with earth, stone, and brick complementing the basic wooden framework. They are often built in a courtyard formation with dwellings on three sides and a decorated screen wall on the entrance side, front courtyard and back courtyard, and one entrance leading to two courtyards. The first type is most basic and most often seen. The rural court-

漂泊驿站
布农小院

关不住阳光
閉語佶夺る

吃
eat

喝
drink

睡
sleep

Sign in Chinese, English
and the local Dongba
language on rural inn

yard formation with dwellings on three sides and a decorated screen wall on the entrance side is a little different
from those found in cities in terms of function. The three
buildings have two stories, and the lower floors of the
main building facing east and the building facing south
are used for living areas with the upper stories used for
storage while the lower floor of the building facing north is
used for sheltering animals with the upper floor used for
storing feed.

The most outstanding characteristic of Naxi dwellings
in Shuhe is that they all have a wide porch in the front,
which they often use as a dining area and for entertaining
guests. The courtyards themselves also have their own
character. Most are covered with paving stones and are
often well landscaped, and many use brick, tile or cobbles
to form large depictions of auspicious Chinese symbols
and characters to make them even more elegant. In addition to daily activities, the courtyards are also used as a
work space and for folk activities.

Leisure in the central room

As the Naxi communities prospered in recent years, villagers have been building new houses. The new houses follow regulations concerning main framework, design and, style to maintain the traditional appearance, but on the inside more and more people are going for modern decoration and modern wall treatment. The houses truly reflect an organic and harmonious blend of ancient and modern.

In order to avoid commercialization of the ancient village, just to the south of the village a beautiful new section has been developed in the ancient style to match the lay of the river and ancient trees. This area is especially designed for locating bars, inns and shops so that the growing crowds of tourists do not disturb the routine lives of the villagers. The local Naxi residents, who are simple, kind, enthusiastic, and hospitable people, are very approachable. Life here is much tranquil and relaxed like olden times than in Lijiang. As you enjoy this return to a more natural lifestyle with the local residents, you too will want this lifestyle to continue this way.

Naxi handicrafts hanging on a wall

Houses on Stilts and the Wind-Rain Bridge: Dong Villages in Liping County, Guizhou Province

T he total area of Liping County in the province of Guizhou is 4,441 square kilometers, and the population is 50,000, 70% of whom belong to the Dong ethnic group. This is the largest concentration of this ethnic minority in the country.

The Dong Area of Scenic and Famous Sites in Liping is located where the provinces of Hunan and Guizhou and the Guangxi Zhuang Autonomous Region meet. The area is chock a block in ethnic culture, natural scenery, historic and cultural sites and sites related to the early history of the CPC (known as "red tour sites"), making tourists reluctant to leave. One of these sites, the Diping Wind-Rain Bridge is a key cultural relic under national protec-

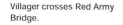

Villager crosses Red Army Bridge.

tion. The Tang'an Dong Village is the only ecological museum of the Dong ethnic minority set up by China and the Kingdom of Norway. Zhaoxing, one of the "six most beautiful ancient rural towns in China," is one of the first group of ten ethnic minority folk culture trial protection sites. The Liping Tiansheng Bridge is the world's largest natural stone arch bridge. When the Dong ethnic minority songs were performed in Paris, people called them "the

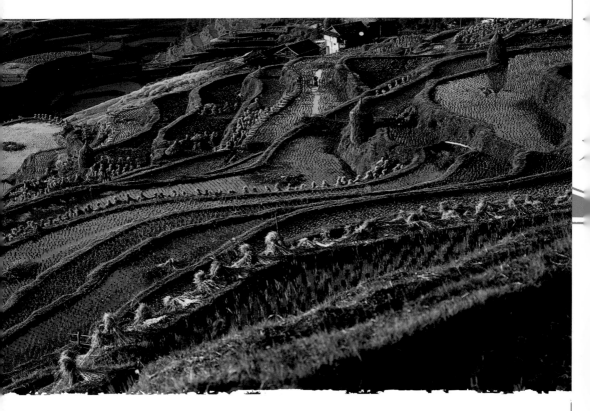

music of a sparkling fountain" and a "hidden civilization." The Liping National Forest Park is a major oxygen generator and an ideal place to look for signs of the ecology of the distant past. Qiaojie Street in the ancient town of Defeng has been compared to a famous painting of the Qing Dynasty depicting scenes along the Grand Canal and the ancient courtyard houses. Walls and eaves in the tourist area of the town all give it an ancient atmosphere. The original site of the "Liping Meeting," a key cultural

Farmland of Tang'an in fall colors

The Dong Village of Zhaoxing

Song and dance of the Dong People

relic under national protection, is listed among the 100 top red tour sites in the country and a site on one of the top 30 red tour routes in the country.

Houses on stilts, which fully take into account the geology and topography of the area, are a major feature of Dong villages in Liping. Guizhou is very mountainous and people say of the area that it's hard to find any level spot longer than a few feet, making construction very difficult. Adapting to local conditions, the Dong people anchor the large wooden support pillars for their houses in the bedrock and then lay the floorboards on top. The area under the house allows good ventilation and keeps the house from becoming too stuffy. The area not only gives them extra living space, but is also well-suited to the local climate, which is rainy and humid. It's like "killing two birds with one stone." The house itself is a two-story wooden structure, usually made of the locally abundant fir, which is very solid. Although mortise and tendon are used in the joints of the building rather than nails, they are exceptionally sturdy. Zhaoxing is the largest and oldest Dong village in the country, and is known as the "number one village of the Dong ethnic group" because it has the most ethnic character of any group of buildings in Liping.

The long-preserved simple appearance of Liping has not yet been over-influenced by commercialization, and you can still get a true feeling for local life here. Just knock on any door and the owner will offer you a room for the night at the low price of just 10 to 20 yuan. You can also eat with the family of the house. The Dong minority sit around a long low narrow table when they eat. On the table they place traditional Dong dishes such as preserved fish, pickled vegetables and squash.

Hakka Civilian Dwellings: Yongding Earthen Houses

The earthen houses of Yongding, Fujian, found in the southern part of the Longyan region, have a very long history. They are unique in character, they are also very large in scale and well crafted. This style of building has been called "a skill unique to China."

Yongding earthen houses are found in two types, square and round. There are 360 round buildings and over 4,000 square ones in Yongding County, Fujian. The round buildings, also known as round stockaded villages, are typical among Hakka residents, and usually consist

Tianluokeng earthen house complex in harmony with the natural scenery

Square Fuyu House

of two to three concentric circles. The outer circle is usually three or four stories tall, contains 100–200 rooms and is over ten meters in height. The first floor is the cooking and dining area, the second floor is for storage and the third and fourth for the bedrooms. The two-story second circle contains 30–50 rooms, usually used for guest rooms. In between is the ancestral hall, a common area used by the several hundred residents for marriages, funerals, and parties. Also included in the compounds are water wells, public baths, and flour mills. The buildings are made from tamped earth obtained locally and do not require reinforced concrete. The walls are 3 meters thick at the base, wide enough to drive a car on, and the lower level walls are 1.5 meters thick, wide enough that a person could lie across it. The wall narrows from bottom to top, but it is usually at least 0.9 meters thick at the top. Wooden planks are used following the inside curve of the walls to form a great number of rooms, and the inner side of the planks form a corridor.

The earthen houses of Yongding, Fujian were mostly built during the Ming (1368–1644) and Qing dynasties

(1644–1911), but their origin goes all the way back to the Western Jin Dynasty (265–316). About that time the Hakka people moved into the area to escape poor agricultural conditions and transformed simple mud brick dwellings into strong and beautiful earthen homes, gradually adding more stories to the structure. Beginning in the middle of the Ming Dynasty, the houses were built bigger and bigger in scale. This kind of structure can not only resist natural disasters such as typhoons and earthquakes, but manmade disasters such as bandit raids as well. Moreover, it allowed the dispersed Hakka people to live together in one place. The people spent most of their days together and got along well, so when threatened by an emergency from the outside they united as one to face the threat.

From ancient times to the 1940s, the earthen houses served as a sturdy bunker for the self-protection of the Hakka people. The main gate of the compound is 20 30cm thick and made of trees with no commercial value plated with iron on the outside and some even have water channels for fire protection above them. The first and second floors of round houses have no windows to pre-

Outside of Zhencheng House

Home of residents of
Zhencheng House

Public sink in an earthen
house

vent enemies from entering. The corridor between the inner and outer walls is sometimes as narrow as one meter wide and runs all the way around the wall. The windows on the outside wall not only provide ventilation and natural light, but also make it convenient to combat outside enemies and protect themselves. Some earthen houses have lookout platforms at the front and two sides of the highest points so they could maintain a lookout for any trouble coming in the distance. In addition to being good for protection and keeping out enemies, the Yongding earthen houses resist earthquakes and fires, keep out wild animals, and allow good ventilation and natural lighting. For good fire protection, the outer walls of some earthen houses are divided into 6, 8, or 10 sections separated by firewalls to prevent a fire from spreading to the whole village. Since the rooms are distributed along the curve of the wall in round houses, there are no dead corners as there are in conventional apartment buildings, making them superior in terms of light and ventilation. The thick walls provide good insulation, so the inside of the rooms is warm in the winter and cool in the summer.

The Zhencheng building, located in Hongkeng Village of Hukeng Township, was built in 1912 and covers an area of 5,000 square meters. It is perched on mountain-like beams and consists of two concentric circles. The outer circle is four stories tall with 48 rooms in each story arranged according to the Eight Trigrams of the Yi Ching. Each section contains 6 rooms and has its own stairway. The ancestral hall of the Zhencheng building is in the form of a stage in front of which stands four stone pillars each nearly 2 meters in circumference and nearly 7 meters in height. The cast iron lattice guardrail on the second floor walkway was shipped to Hukeng Village from Shanghai. Over the door to the main hall are the words of an early Nationalist president, Li Yuanhong (1864–1928). The Zhencheng building was displayed along with the Yonghegong Lamasery and Great Wall at the World's Fair of Architectural Models held in Los Angeles in April 1986.

Residence of a Shanxi Businessman: the Grand Courtyard of Qiao Family

U
nlike the villages and towns we visited on the countryside tour above, this estate only has one household, but the importance of this household cannot be compared with that of an ordinary town or village.

The grand courtyard of Qiao family was formerly the private residence of the very wealthy Qiao family who were members of the business class of Shanxi and is located in the exact center of Qiaojiapu Village in Qixian County of Shanxi Province. The estate covers a total area of 8,724 square meters, 3,870 of which are occupied by buildings. It is divided into 6 main courtyards further divided into 20 smaller courtyards containing 313 rooms. Looking at the estate from the air it can be seen that the arrangement forms an auspicious "double happiness" Chinese character. The estate is a completely enclosed

A unique courtyard

Brick wall and passage
in a courtyard

group of buildings in the form of a bunker. Three sides
adjoin streets and all four sides are enclosed behind brick
walls that are over 10 meters tall, at the top of which are
daughter walls with lookout windows to hide behind and
maintain a lookout in case of attack to ensure security
and give the outside an imposing appearance. The grand
courtyard of Qiao family is well designed and well built,
and fully reflects the unique style of Qing Dynasty residential buildings. It is an incomparable architectural treasure that experts and scholars call "a bright pearl among
northern residential buildings" and others praise it saying, "See the Forbidden City to see how the royal family
lived and see the grand courtyard of Qiao family to see a
fine example of how common people lived."

There are three large courtyards at the northern end
of the estate, from east to west called the old courtyard,
northwest courtyard and study courtyard in accordance
with tradition. The three large courtyards at the southern
end are called the southeast courtyard, the southwest
courtyard, and new courtyard. The names of the six
courtyards at the two ends of the estate indicate the order
of the buildings. A perfectly straight stone-paved path 80
meters in length divides the courtyards into a southern
row and a northern row. The ends of the paths where
they meet the outer wall are protected by small hills.
Each courtyard has 4 main buildings, gatehouse, night

Exquisite handicraft of board pictures

guard tower, and six lookout pavilions. All the rooms are connected by a path on the roof for the use of guard patrols. The grand courtyard of Qiao family is famous worldwide, not only for the grand and imposing appearance of the buildings in the estate, but even more for the excellent workmanship evident in every brick, tile, stone, and piece of wood. Moreover, there are engraved bricks, wood carvings, and paintings to be seen throughout the six large courtyards. Looking at the overall appearance, the estate appears grand and imposing, well ordered with a strict arrangement and carefully considered architecture; it is at once static and dynamic. Not only is the overall appearance aesthetically pleasing, but each building also has its own unique character. The more than 140 chimneys on the buildings each have their own unique style. All the pavilions, platforms, buildings, and raised pavilions throughout the estate have engraved beams, painted posts, and other eloquent decorations fully demonstrating the fine craftsmanship of the working people of ancient China. A more valuable example of this is no-

Picturesque mosaic of rooftops and unique chimneys

where to be found.

Construction on the grand courtyard of Qiao family began in the 20th year of the reign of the Qing Emperor Qianlong (1756) and has since been enlarged twice and renovated once. Nearly two centuries passed between the time construction began and the time it attained its current appearance. Although this is a long period of time, the estate has retained its original character through enlargement and renovation. The overall character of the estate is uniform despite the mixture of styles.

In 1985 the Qixian County People's Government turned this ancient residence into the Qixian County Museum of Ethnic Customs, which officially opened to the public on November 1, 1986. The museum displays over 5,000 valuable relics to provide a concise picture of the folk customs of central Shanxi. They include rural customs, the rites and ceremonies of life, climatic conditions, clothing, dietary and housing habits, ways of doing commerce, and folk handicrafts. Also on display are historical documents concerning the Qiao family, Qiao family jewelry, and special topic video displays. Over 8 million foreign and domestic visitors have passed through the museum's doors since it opened. The movie *Raise the Red Lantern High* directed by Zhang Yimou further increased the fame of the grand courtyard of Qiao family.

Xidi and Hongcun : Ancient Villages in Huizhou

It was decided at the 24th Meeting of the World Heritage Committee held in Cairns, Australia, on November 30, 2001 to add the two ancient Anhui villages of Xidi and Hongcun to the list of world heritage sites.

Hongcun

Hongcun lies 11 kilometers northwest of the county seat of Yixian in southern Anhui Province and 65 kilometers from Tunxi, location of the airport for Huangshan Mountain tourists. Construction on the village began during the Northern Song Dynasty (960–1127), nearly 1,000 years ago. The ancient people of Hongcun were unique. They were at the forefront of the science of bionics, a unique talent they demonstrated in planning and building this buffalo-shaped village and manmade water system. The water system is designed in the image of a buffalo. The system brings in fresh spring water through the "buffalo's intestine" that then runs in front of every household so that "though the river is far, every household has fresh water at their doorstep." When the water flows from the "intestine" and enters the village, it goes

White clouds in a blue sky over Moon Pond in Hongcun Village

Residents of Hongcun Village lead horse carts on a stone path along South Lake.

into the crescent-shaped pool called the "buffalo's stomach." After filtering, the water then makes its way around to all the households in the village and then out of the village to the South Lake, known as the "buffalo's belly." It is then filtered one more time before releasing the water back into the riverbed. The overall layout of the village resembles a water buffalo lifting its head and holding up its hooves. The building of this kind of water system has been called a skill that is unique among the ancient villages of China. It has attracted experts from Japan, the US, and Germany to observe and carefully study it.

The village contains 140-some well-preserved examples of Ming and Qing dynasty residential buildings. One of the most representative of these is the beautiful and imposing Chengzhi Hall, a Qing Dynasty residence called the "Forbidden City of Common People's Houses," which could be called the best in southern Anhui Province. The extremely well crafted groups of wooden carvings in the residence known as "One Hundred Children at Play during the Lantern Festival" and "Tang Emperor Suzong Invites Officials to a Banquet" and the stone carvings in the windows without glass are exquisite beyond compare. The world renowned architect Ieoh Ming Pei once remarked, "The buildings and cultural relics of Hongcun in Yixian County are national treasures." The varied appearances of the buildings in the village combine with the lake and the mountains to form beautiful scenes wherever one looks. From the natural environment outside of the village to the water system, streets, buildings, and even the interiors of the houses in the village, everything in the village has been preserved as it was in the ancient village with practically no trace of

the modernity. With its unique appearance and supreme beauty, Hongcun has been called the "Chinese village in the picture."

Xidi

Xidi lies 8 kilometers east of Yixian County. Construction began during the Huangyou years (1049–1054) of the Northern Song nearly 1,000 years ago. Yixian County was once part of the ancient Huizhou and was located in the western part of Huizhou Prefecture. It became famous because of the posthouse that was located there. The natural environment and scenery of Xidi are like those described by Tao Yuanming in his *Story of the Peach Blossom Valley* and Xidi is known as "Home in the Peach Blossom Valley." Experts and scholars call Xidi "a concise picture of traditional Chinese culture" and "museum of Chinese homes of the Ming and Qing dynasties."

Xidi is famous throughout China for its longstanding and brilliant traditional culture, outstanding Hui style homes of the Ming and Qing dynasties, simple and pure folk customs, and the extremely well crafted Hui style wooden carvings, engraved bricks, and stone sculptures. The most unique residences include Daifudi, Yingfutang,

Xidi after the rain brings out the contrast between white walls and black roof tiles.

Exquisite and beautiful
stone sculpture of Xidi

Hengrentang, Xiyuan, and Ruiyuting. Most of the houses
were built near water and have exquisitely and intricately
carved pointed arches over the doors, curving walls with
stone carving windows, each with its own unique character, and stone benches, wells, and stone block bridges
in the streets. These buildings and objects all preserve the
appearance they had during the Ming and Qing dynasties. The overall outward appearance of the village is in
harmony with the local topography, topology, and natural
scenery. It is very aesthetically pleasing and embodies the
special flavor of the ancient villages of southern Anhui.

Many of the buildings in the village use black marble
and two streams run through the village. Along with the
99 high-walled lanes and unique residences, they make

the tourists feel as though in a maze.

At the main entrance to the village is a five-story stone memorial arch with three rooms and four columns erected in the sixth year of the Ming Emperor Wanli (1578) called the "Hu Wenguang Memorial Gateway," also known as the "Xidi Memorial Gateway." The gateway, which is imposing and carefully built, is an obvious symbol of the status of the Hu family, as well as a fine example of Ming Dynasty Hui style stone gateways and the symbol of Xidi.

The village also has the grand and imposing Lüfutang Hall built during the reign of Qing Emperor Kangxi (1661–1722) in the lobby of which is a couplet that is a perfect melding of academia and architecture.

The fertile ground of Xidi has produced a number of famous and important officials and business magnates, including Ming Dynasty Prefectural Governor Hu Wenguang, Qing Dynasty grade II official Hu Shangzeng, and the extremely successful Qing Dynasty businessman Hu Guansan.

Gateway of Xidi

Cuandixia Village : Ancient Village in Western Beijing

Cuandixia Village, also known as Mingqing Village and Guji Village, is the site of an ancient mountain retreat located 90 kilometers outside of Beijing on the ancient route leading west out of the city. Cuandixia Village, which retains the ancient character

This complicated Chinese character is the most concise indicator of the village.

of the Ming and Qing dynasties, is situated to the north up against a mountain and faces south. The village consists of a patchwork of tall and short buildings and has been called the "Potala Palace" of western Beijing. The overall layout of the village is perfectly in harmony with the natural surroundings. There are 70 courtyard houses on the north-south axis centered on Longtou (Dragon's

Head) Mountain, and the heights of the houses follow the contour of the mountain in the shape of a fan going down the mountain. Looking at the village from a distant hill to the south, the village looks very much like a traditional fan-shaped ingot of silver or gold and at the same time resembles the yin and yang diagram found at the center of the Eight Trigrams. Surrounded by mountains, the village has a typical mountain village environment of mountains and streams that can be clearly seen from afar. On November 27, 2003 the village was named for inclusion in the first group of Chinese cultural and historical villages by the Ministry of Construction and the State Cultural Relics Bureau.

Cuandixia is the residence of the Han clan. The first of the family to arrive came from Shanxi during the reign of

Panoramic view of Cuandixia Village

Bumper crop of corn, primitive sun-drying

the Ming Emperor Yongle (1403–1424) over 400 years ago. The village of Cuandixia (meaning below the bottom of Cuan) is located down from the Ming Dynasty military mountain pass of Cuanli'ankou, and hence its name.

A total of 76 courtyards have been preserved containing 656 residences in the village, which occupies an area of about 10,000 square meters. The structure of the village is careful, precise and rational, a jumble of styles with an overarching theme. A winding street divides the village into upper and lower sections. Architectural details such as the stone walls, arched gateways, decorated screen walls, engraved bricks, stone carvings and wood sculptures, give the village the feeling of the villages of southern China while retaining the feeling of broad magnificence of the large courtyard houses of northern China. The village has retained its original appearance and the character of a Ming or Qing dynasty village in spite of drastic changes that have taken place during its centuries of existence. It is the first fairly well preserved group of ancient dwellings in a northern mountain village discovered in the country. People say, "For the folk customs

Zhouzhuang: A Town of Rivers and Lakes in Southern China

Zhouzhuang lies 38 kilometers to the southeast of the city of Suzhou, Jiangsu Province and covers an area of 0.47 square kilometers. It was known as Yaocheng in ancient times when it was the fief of the crown prince Yao and was part of the state of Wu during the Spring and Autumn Period. Zhouzhuang, also known as Zhenbanli, was founded when Zhou Digong, a local resident and fervent believer in Buddhism during the Northern Song Dynasty, contributed his residence and 200 *mu* of good agricultural land to the temple. To show

Bird's-eye view of Zhouzhuang

their gratitude, the local people changed the name to Zhouzhuang.

Zhouzhuang has been known as the "Land of Rivers and Lakes" since ancient times. Deng Lake, Baixian Lake, Dianshan Lake, and Nan Lake, as well as more than 30 rivers, are found in the vicinity and its round shape resembles a lotus leaf floating on the water. The peaceful environment of natural waters and unique and pleasing scenery and simple folk customs make it a typical southern Chinese region and an Oriental treasure. Zhouzhuang has been put on UNESCO's preliminary list of world cultural heritage sites and has been awarded the Dubai prize for the best example of a good living environment, the UN prize for outstanding achievements in the protection of the world's cultural heritage in the Asia-Pacific Region and a US government prize. It was also named as

Street market along the river

the world's most attractive region of lakes and rivers and listed among the first group of 10 towns named by the Chinese government for their historical and cultural significance.

There are four main river channels running through the town of Zhouzhuang and smaller streams crisscross the town forming a pound sign. The streets follow the course of the rivers as they crisscross the town, with the fronts of the houses facing the street and the backs to the river, thereby fully preserving the ancient flavor of the town and the old feel and flavor of an ancient town in the Ming and Qing dynasties. The town contains nearly a hundred buildings from the period of the Ming and Qing dynasties, over 60 engraved brick doorway arches and 24

Most famous scene of Zhouzhuang—Double Bridge

Street performers

stone bridges over the straight and narrow river channels (including 10 from the period of the Yuan (1271–1368), Ming, and Qing dynasties). All this forms a typical picture of southern China as in the saying, "small bridges, flowing water and homes."

Construction of the houses takes into account their watery environment. The simple unadorned houses line the rivers in the large courtyard compounds throughout the town. Each bridge, each street, each temple and every room, the azul water, blue skies, green trees, stone streets all preserve the feeling of ancient Zhouzhuang, which is the reason the town has been the delight of Chinese and foreign artists from the distant past to the present. Wu Guanzhong, a famous ancient painter, said, "Huangshan Mountain is a concentrated reflection of the beauty of the country's mountains and streams, and Zhouzhuang is a concentrated reflection of the beauty of China's regions of rivers and lakes." The houses of the town also have a great amount of cultural significance. Western Jin Dynasty literary expert Zhang Han and Tang Dynasty poets Liu Yuxi and Lu Guimeng once lived here. Modern cultural personalities such as Liu Yazi and Chen Qubing have also

visited and stayed here. Contemporary Chinese painter Chen Yifei was inspired by the Double Bridge in Zhouzhuang to create the famous oil painting called, *Memories of the Hometown*, which was later featured on a UN first day cover issue. This was Zhouzhuang's road to greater fame.

The thousand-year-old town of Zhouzhuang is carrying on the poetic and picturesque feeling of beautiful southern China, and its quiet grandeur welcomes all guests who come here. Zhouzhuang has now introduced demonstrations of traditional crafts such as making textiles, iron forging, and bamboo weaving, as well as folk performances such as lion and dragon dances to help tourists better appreciate the picturesque "small bridges, running water, and homes" in southern China as well as enjoy the rich cultural attractions and unique folk customs.

The Immigrant Town of Nianbadu

Development of Nianbadu began in 1931 in a basin in the Xianxia Mountains where the three provinces of Zhejiang, Fujian and Jiangxi meet. The town is surrounded by mountains covered in trees. To the south is the Xiaogangling Reservoir, which feeds the Nianbadu Creek flowing from north to south, creating a beautiful scene. Nianbadu was important commercially and militarily in ancient times. Many military personnel and traders passed through the town during its 1,000 years of history, leaving their trace in the 142 different surnames and nine dialects and a wide variety of folk customs and folk arts in the town and producing an "im-

Door lintel of ancient residence of Jiang Shoujin

Sun-drenched crops in an old courtyard

"immigrant culture" in the town different from that of other ancient towns in southern China. Thus people call it a "cultural enclave" and "small immigrant town."

The major families of the ancient town include the families of Cao, Jiang, Yang, and Jin, which are grouped in clans. A total of 36 large ancient courtyard compounds have been entirely preserved. Standing on the old streets, the most obvious and unique feature is the lintels of the doorways, usually in the form of an arched doorway, with overhead beam, rafter, and eaves. Every part is decorated with carefully crafted wood carvings in the form of auspicious symbols.

Because the ancient town was protected by surrounding mountain passes, it was seldom subject to attack. Two sections of ancient commercial streets about one kilometer in length and 36 common dwellings have been fairly well preserved. One ancient street in the town that was built in the 19th century is so narrow that a modern car cannot pass through it, but the two sides of the street are tightly packed with stores and shops. The interior of the houses are neat and clean and in the doorways hang traditional signs. The street stretches 1.5 kilometers in length and reflects the rich cultural atmosphere of the Ming and Qing dynasties. Over 10 public buildings and more than 20 common residences have basically preserved the architectural appearance of the Ming and Qing dynasties. The architectural styles are different from the style of diverting rainwater to the courtyard of the Zhejiang-Anhui region of rivers and lakes, blending the style of wood carvings from Zhejiang, the engraved bricks of Anhui and the stucco walls of Jiangxi and architectural styles of the Hakka people of northern Fujian and even Roccoco style.

The stone Fengxi Bridge

In particular, the two "Wenchang Pavilions," one large and one small, contain frescoes with extremely high cultural value and stone inscriptions, which are seldom seen in the country. For these reasons they have been called the "museum of folk architecture."

In the ancient town of Nianbadu, with its ancient paths, impregnable pass, small bridges, peasant houses, and flowing water, ancient streets follow the winding path of the brook with a patchwork of ancient buildings of various heights. The major scenic spots in the town include "Shui'an Liangfeng," "Fengxi Wangyue," "Zhengshou Qinglan," and "Longshan Muma."

Old temple is used for activities of senior citizens today.

Kaiping, Guangdong: East Meets West in the Diaolou

Kaiping is located in the western part of the Pearl River Delta in the hills and plains. It is home to an exotic architectural treasure— the Diaolou (watchtower house).

Beginning in the Ming Dynasty, the local peasants, worried about their remote location, pooled their resources to build high imposing watchtower houses in the village to resist bandits and floods. At the end of the Opium War in 1840, many villagers were forced to leave the village to seek other livelihoods, crossing the sea to America in great numbers to work as laborers. At the beginning of the last century, many overseas Chinese, though they had been successfully working overseas for a number of years, still longed for their homeland and gradually

Watchtowers of Zili Village

began returning home. Conditions in the country at the time were very unsettled, with warlords and bandits controlling different regions of the country. The only way the returning villagers could protect themselves was to turn their homes into tall imposing watchtowers. The returning Chinese had spent most of their lives overseas and had been greatly affected by foreign art and culture to which they were exposed, so the watchtowers they built showed strong influences from classical Western architecture. The reason Kaiping became such a thriving place at the beginning of the last century was due to hard labor of those overseas Chinese, which also greatly enriched the cultural content and value of the Kaiping Diaolou.

During its most prosperous period, there were over 3,000 watchtowers in the county of Kaiping. Stretching dozens of kilometers from Shuikou to Baihe and from

Risheng Watchtower and Yiyun Watchtower

47

Unbroken scene of
terraces of Chikan Town

period of the Republic of China (1923–1925) by Huang
Bixiu, a private Hong Kong banker and medical supply
magnate. Ruishi Tower is located to the east of Jinjiang
Tower on the main axis running through the residences of
the village and is a good example of a residential watchtower. The whole building has the feel of a medieval Ital-
ian castle. But while the sides of the building use Western
style window sills like porticoes with carved plaster,
among the many images are traditional Chinese auspicious characters such as prosperity, riches, happiness, and
long life. Underneath the Western exterior is the rich flavor of traditional Chinese culture and traditional Chinese
style.

The Diaolou of Kaiping was inscribed World Heritage
status by the 31st World Heritage Committee meeting on
June 28, 2007.

Jiaju Tibetan Village, the Most Beautiful Village in China

Jiaju Tibetan Village is located in Danba County in the Hengduan Mountains of western Sichuan. It is situated on a mountain slope 500 to 600 meters higher than the town of Danba, which is already quite high. A whitewater river, the Dajin River, flows through the valley below the villages and then into the Dadu River.

The term jiaju in Tibetan means a group of 100 or more households. Jiaju Tibetan Village covers an area of five square kilometers and is occupied by 149 households of Jiarong Tibetan people, whose houses are scattered up and down the mountain slope nearly a thousand meters.

Tibetan village in the spring.

manship. Each family has its own home. Most of them face south. Some are in clusters of three to five, and others stand alone, apart from the others. The houses are all built in a similar style that is adapted to the terrain and reflects the Tibetan culture. They all have gardens in front and are surrounded by fruit trees, and all this combines to make Jiaju Tibetan Village a beautiful mountain locale. The mountain slope rising from the river in the valley to the mountain ridge is studded with outcroppings and recesses. And it is in the recesses where most of the houses are situated. So they are partially hidden by the orchards and fields and blend in harmoniously with the mountain landscape of flowing streams and snow-capped peaks, stretching out with all the aesthetic appeal of a classical landscape painting.

Bird's-eye view of a Tibetan village

The houses are built in the style of ancient blockhouses

Preserved meat hanging from carved beams and painted rafters

and are called blockhouse homes. Originally blockhouses and houses were built according to different styles, but over time, the two styles merged seamlessly. From the outside, the houses can be seen to have characteristics of both styles. Around the upper part of the building they all have painted bands of yellow, black, and white. This is a unique characteristic of Jiarong homes. What's most unique about the houses is that at the four corners of the roof there are miniature white stone towers representing deities of the four cardinal directions. The towers have sutra streamers attached to them, which give the roofs the appearance of half moons. Every year during the spring and fall worship rituals and during sacrifices to their ancestors, the Jiarong people offer sacrifices at these miniature towers.

All the walls in the village buildings are made from

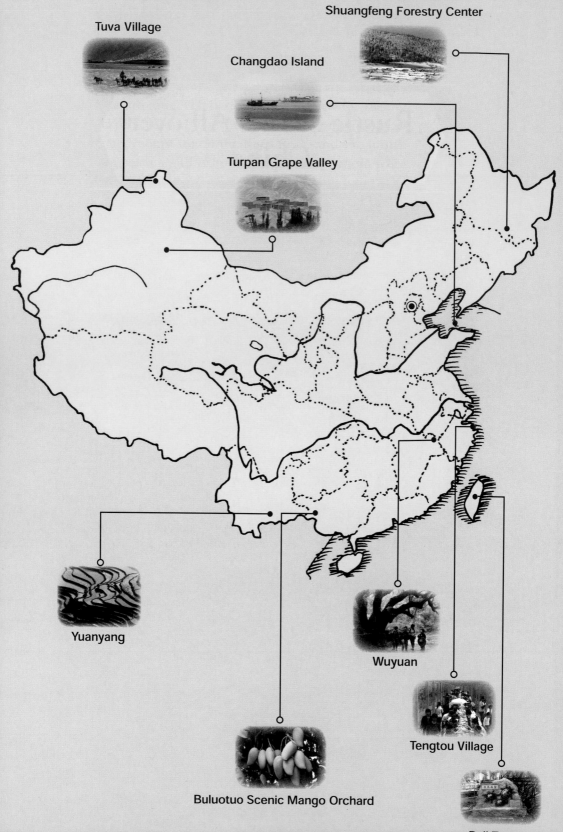

Tuva Village

Shuangfeng Forestry Center

Changdao Island

Turpan Grape Valley

Yuanyang

Wuyuan

Buluotuo Scenic Mango Orchard

Tengtou Village

Puli Town

Wuyuan: Possibly the Most Beautiful Countryside

Wuyuan is a county in Jiangxi Province with a long history that formerly belonged to Anhui. Fortunately, Wuyuan has preserved all the charm of ancient Huizhou. It is a brilliant green patch of nature and bright pearl of ancient culture on the Huangshan Mountain-Jingdezhen-Lushan Mountain route so popular with international tourists. Wuyuan is rich in resources for ecotourism, with 2,400 square kilometers of forested land, accounting for 82% of the total area of the county. People say of the area that it is "8.5 parts mountains, 1 part fields and 0.5 parts waterways and manors."

Beautiful scenery can be found wherever one looks in Wuyuan as though it were a giant park. People call it "the most beautiful countryside in China" and "the last Shangri-La." Wuyuan includes a rich store of famous and ancient sites such as the well preserved ancient villages of Jiangwan, Wangkou, Sixi, and Likeng. The green mountains with their lush vegetation and mountain streams

Spring scenery in Jiangling Village, Xitou Township: the mountain covered with canola in bloom and the ancient Huizhou-style residences form a beautiful picture.

The gorgeous scenery of Wuyuan in the winter with the thick forests, plastered walls and black-tiled roofs is like a watercolor painted by a master.

A recently discovered ancient screen wall in Hongcun Village of Qinghua Town created near the end of the Ming and beginning of the Qing dynasty that perfectly combines wood carving, brick sculpture and stone sculpture. It is composed of three parts, the outer ring, the middle ring and the inner ring. The outer ring is carved of camphorwood and is about 15cm wide in the shape of clouds. The middle ring is made of dark green brick and is decorated with eight kinds of flowers and leaves: plum blossoms, magnolias, peonies, lotuses, osmanthus, pear blossoms, chrysanthemum flowers and peach blossoms. The inner ring is made of carved brick and stone.

alongside the plaster walls, black tiles and upturned eaves of the houses form a perfect picture of tranquility and harmony between man and nature. The Ming and Qing buildings with their plaster walls, black tiles and upturned eaves, plus the stone paths and bridges and tier after tier of terraced fields make the visitor feel as though he is totally immersed in a traditional Chinese painting.

Wuyuan not only has beautiful scenery that rivals a painting, but has also long been known as the "literary place" and has a thriving literary feel. In ancient times it was said, "the sound of reading coming from the straw huts, people putting down their work to sit for an examination." From the Song to the Qing Dynasty, 550 people from the village passed the highest imperial examination and 2,665 people served as officials. An old saying goes, "A household had nine members passing the imperial examination and four of the country's six ministers had studied here." Wuyuan scholars and authors produced over 3,100 works, 172 of which have been included in the *Com-*

Spring rain in Wuyuan

plete Library of the Four Branches of Literature. The people of an area are influenced by the local conditions, and the literary and academic spirit has continued here for generations, producing many outstanding persons, such as the writer Zhu Bian, the philosopher, educator and Neo-Confucianist Zhu Xi, Ming Dynasty seal carver He Zhen, Qing Dynasty Confucian classicist Jiang Yong, scientist Qi Yanhuai, "father of the railway," Zhan Tianyou, and modern medical expert Cheng Menxue. All of them have emerged from Wuyuan and gone out to China and the world.

Products of Wuyuan are famous in China and overseas. The local products, typified by four colors (red, green, white, and black) and four things from the past (ancient villages, ancient caves, ancient buildings, and ancient culture), have a long history and unique cultural character. Red is for the "treasure of the water," the purse red carp. This fish, which has been selected for state banquets, is tender and flavorful, but in addition to eating it, the fish is used in medicines and in carp ponds for their

visual beauty. Green is for Wuyuan green tea, which has become famous far and wide for its color, good fragrance, good viscosity, and pleasing taste. Black is for the dragon tail inkstones, which are famous around the world because of the way they "ring like copper, have the color of iron, have a hard and smooth surface, and are excellent for making ink." White is for the Jiangwan snow pears, which are large, fleshy, crisp, sweet, and flavorful, a premium fruit variety. The area is also known for folk handicrafts such as Jialu decorative umbrellas, woven bamboo, embroidery, wooden carvings and root sculptures, as well as for Qinghuawu liquor, special fish dish, shitake mushrooms, dried bamboo shoots and dried wild vegetables, all of which make excellent gifts for friends and relatives.

Wuyuan is rich in folk arts. The elegant Anhui opera is one of the sources of Beijing opera. The ancient Nuo dance has been called the "living fossil of ancient dance, the Taige art of Jialu Village is said to be "a skill unique to China" and the unique tea ceremony is enchanting.

Exorcise dance performance

The Ming and Qing buildings of Likeng Village

Shuangfeng Forestry Center: Snow Village in the Northeast

Shuangfeng Forestry Center, also called Snow Village, is located in Hailin Prefecture, Heilongjiang, a four-hour drive west of the city of Hailin. In recent years, its fame has grown by leaps and bounds as it has won a number of international awards for its incomparable scenery. The novel *Tracks in the Snowy Forest*, which tells the tale of Yang Zirong taking Tiger Mountain by strategy and liberating Jiapigou, was set in this area.

Snow Village has a unique geographical setting. When

Snowy forest

Shuangfeng Town and its ski resort

you raise your head, all you see is trees. This is the home of red and white pines, and it contains a 297-hectare primeval red pine forest whose trees average 400 years old and more than 30 meters high. The wind soughs through the forest like thunder, setting the verdant trees in motion. The Hailang River, the largest tributary of the Mudan River, has its source here, pouring forth in a constant flow. In the summer people come here for rafting, camping, exploring the forest, and gathering mountain flora. In the winter, this is the best place for people to go skiing or otherwise enjoy the snow and watch professional skiers perform.

Snow Village's climate is affected by the nearby mountains, and every winter it starts to snow early and accumulates to a depth of about two meters. The snow season lasts nearly seven months there, and it is widely agreed that it gets the most snow of any place in China. One reason Snow Village is so famous is because the quality

Courtyard at the foot of the
mountain

Horse-drawn sleighs

of the snow is excellent. Cold air from Siberia mixes with warm air from the Sea of Japan to form translucent, wet snow that accumulates around the objects underneath like an endless variety of mushrooms and gives a distinctive cast to houses built in the traditional local style. Here, you can not only personally experience the charms of snow but also deeply appreciate the feeling the locals have of living with the snow, relying on it for their livelihood and being totally surrounded by a pure white landscape.

The pure white snow piles reflect the shape of the objects beneath and take the shape of an arc on roofs of houses.

Snow Village, where the forestry center is located, is very small, and if you go there in winter, you can see only one road covered in snow. All the village streets are regularly shoveled clean, with walls of snow rising on either side. They're very narrow and wind around past everyone's home. The vehicles in the village include trucks for hauling lumber as well as horse-drawn sleighs and dogsleds. Most of the people in the village are employees of the forestry center and their families. For the most part they no longer rely on lumbering for a living, but spend most of their time gardening and offering hospitality to tourists. When tourists come to Snow Village, the locals warmly welcome them into their homes, where the tourists are served natural foods grown locally, sleep on heated brick beds that are a distinctive feature of homes in Northeast China, and get taken to see the sights in dogsleds. Visitors are always mesmerized by the fresh, crisp air after a snowstorm and the simple and pure temperament of the local people.

The homes in Snow Village are all old wooden houses, and when it snows, they look like short stout mushrooms that just sprung up, standing there lazily. The houses all have a small garden right out the door surrounded by a picket fence that follows a line like in a freehand charcoal drawing. When the residents hang their silver coats on the pickets to dry, they look like ice cream bars about to melt and the bare pickets between the clothes by contrast look like cakes. Strolling through Snow Village looking at the snow mushrooms, cakes and ice cream bars, you get the feeling of being transported into a painting of winter landscape. Snow Village looks even more beautiful at night. The villagers all hang large red lanterns from the eaves of their houses, and the light from the lanterns magically transforms the landscape so it seems like clouds have descended from the sky and are floating all around.

Tuva Village beside Kanasi Lake

Tuva Village is located in the area of Kanasi Lake deep in the Altai Mountains of Burqin County, Xinjiang. The narrow canyon between two peaks is just big enough for 80-some dwellings. The Tuva people have made their living from raising sheep and cattle and hunting for many generations. Deep in the dense forest, they seldom have contact with the outside world and have clung to their traditional lifestyle. Since the famous scenic spot of Kanasi Lake northwest of the village was opened up to tourists, people have been gradually learning about this tranquil and beautiful village.

The Tuva people are herders who belong to one of the

Tuva archery competition →

Tuva Village

oldest ethnic minorities in northern China. The total current Tuva population of Kanasi Village and the neighboring Hemu Village is a little over 2,900. The Tuva language, which belongs to the family of Turkic languages, is one of the rarest currently used languages in China, though Mongolian has become more common in schools for Tuva people. The Tuva people believe in Tibetan Buddhism and most still believe in shamanism. They customarily celebrate the traditional Mongolian holiday of Aobao, as well as the local Zoulu (Beginning of Winter) festival and the Han Chinese New Year and Lantern Festival.

The Tuva language does not have a written form and therefore has left no written history and local records say very little about them. A common local opinion holds that they are descendants of people Ghengis Khan left behind on his westward march. Looking at the modern Tuva people, it can be seen that they physically resemble Mongolian people, and that their clothing, accessories and daily habits are basically the same as well. In terms of

Tuva Village household

religious belief, the Tuva and Mongolians both currently believe in Lamaism and both have retained some customs from shamanism. The great majority of Tuva people believe they are connected to Ghengis Khan and all Tuva homes display his picture.

Tuva herdsman and his horses

The dwellings of the Tuva people are unusual. They are all made of wood and a single color. In addition, because the small wooden cabins are all perfectly lined up, it gives the village a very neat and orderly look. Moreover, the houses are all surrounded by picket fences making the village strongly resemble a village in northern Europe. Behind the Tuva village stands Friendship Peak on the Sino-Russian border with its snowy peaks. The village arises every day at the crack of dawn, and the rays of the sun turn the forests of white birch trees on the slopes to gold while the cattle and sheep casually mill about,

The only school in the Kanasi region—Tuva Primary School.

making a fascinating scene. Wooden bridges, running water, villages, white birch, cattle ship constitute the most beautiful scene here.

The Kanasi Tuva Village and Kanasi Lake complement each other. The area is surrounded by verdant mountains and limpid streams, and the beautiful environment is a unique attraction of the scenes of humanity and ethnic character of the Kanasi tourist region. Tourists coming from afar can not only appreciate the exotic beauty of the natural scenery, but also visit the natives of the village of the Tuva people and learn about the unique folk customs of the Tuva. The Tuva often say of the area that it has "seven months of winter and five months of summer." Winter snow cuts off the village from the outside and they often fill their days drinking. Someone once took a survey that indicated the people of the village consume 45 tons of alcohol during the winter.

The Terraced Fields of the Hani People in Yuanyang

Yuanyang County is located on the south bank of the Honghe River in southern Yunnan. There are no level areas; the topography is all tall mountains cut by deep valleys. The terraced fields and sea of clouds form a majestic and beautiful scene and its unique character has led people to call them "the heavenly terraced fields of Yuanyang." Over 360,000 *mu* of terraced fields are distributed across the mountain slopes in a vast and daunting array of color that fills the scene in all directions. Yuanyang is rich in tourist venues and is the core area of the Honghe River Hani terraced fields now pending recognition as a world heritage site.

The Hani people first moved into the area at the end of the Sui and beginning of the Tang dynasties. They started converting wasteland by terracing fields to form rice pad-

Terraced fields under clouds and blue sky

The terraced fields of Yuanyang were set up on slopes ranging from 15 to 75 degrees. There are up to 3,000 terraces on the slopes of this one mountain, forming a scene that is rare in both China and abroad.

dies. In the 12 plus centuries since then, generations of the Hani have toiled and used their surprising wisdom and willpower to carve out thousands of terraced fields from the wasteland on the surrounding mountain sides. On the larger mountains they carved out hundreds of water canals and dry channels. The canals and dry channels look like silver belts tightly wrapped around the mountains. They collect the many large and small streams of water flowing down the mountain and resolve the crucial problem of watering the fields. The fields of Yuanyang are irrigated by streams that flow down from the top of the mountain all year long. The local people made the fields according to the topography and geology of the plot so that the many tiers of fields follow the shape of the mountain and zigzag as they go up the mountain. They take advantage of the fact that water flows downhill to gather the continuous flow of water and direct it to the fields to form an automatic irrigation network. From top to bottom, Yuanyang is a mountainous scenic area with a perfectly balanced ecological system consisting of four phases—forests, water system, village, and fields.

The technique of converting wasteland on the slopes of areas like this with mountains of various altitudes into terraced fields began to reach China and Southeast Asia in the 14th century. The Hani people went one step further by turning area of Ailao Mountain into a series of artworks. As a result, a Ming Dynasty emperor called the Hani "miraculous mountain sculptors" and this name has

Every year after the Chinese New Year, the terraced fields begin to collect water so that planting can begin. Water buffaloes are the main agricultural tools since it would be impossible to use mechanical equipment.

been handed down to the present.

The terraced fields of the Hani people of Yuanyang are a large lively and dynamic system, as it has been since ancient times. It is a human creation that harmoniously combines nature and human society in the form of the Hani people blending with the natural environment of Ailao Mountain. It is also a combination of history and culture with nature. The rows and rows of terraced fields go up the sides of the mountain like a stairway reaching to the sky. During periods of fog, a great many of the fields are hidden from view and the scene resembles a mysterious ladder extending from earth up into the heavens.

Seven different ethnic groups, the Hani, Yi, Dai, Yao, Miao, Zhuang and Han reside in Yuanyang, a typical mountain area with an ethically mixed population. The brilliant mixture of ethnic cultures, with the Hani terraced field culture as most prominent feature, lends a strong ethnic culture to the area. The traditional local festivals such as the Longstreet Banquet and October Festival of the Hani, the Torch Festival of the Yi and the Dance Flower Festival of the Miao are elegant and colorful.

The terraced fields of the Hani people of Yuanyang are the product of the history of the culture of rice paddy and

Terraced fields in the midst of heavy forest

crop cultivation, and represent the crystallization of the wisdom of ethnic minority groups through a long period of survival and development. The Hani people living in the mountains created the terraced fields to meet the requirements for their survival and development and managed to maintain a balance between human development and nature through a long period of agricultural cultivation. This then is the far-reaching significance of the terraced fields of the Hani ethnic group: smoothly integrating human society with nature.

Puli Town, Nantou County

The town of Puli is located in the geographical center of Taiwan in the northern part of Nantou County, 61 kilometers southeast of Taichung and 17 kilometers north of Sun Moon Lake. There is not only beautiful natural scenery, but also unique recreational agriculture.

In order to help farmers overcome the challenges presented by the rules imposed on agriculture by the WTO, the Puli Agricultural Association set up the Tourist Service Center and developed the policy of setting up a leisure agricultural plot for each village to take advantage of the unique mountain water and closely integrate the natural scenery with agriculture. On the one hand, the policy will provide tourists with a comprehensive high-quality agricultural tour and on the other assist farmers in developing high-quality and interesting leisure agriculture and boosting sales of local produce and processed agricultural products. Leisure agriculture represents

Entrance to the zone's flower conservatory

Sign to the Museum of
Entomology

a change from traditional agricultural production by strengthening utilization of agricultural land and natural resources to develop a new service industry that makes use of agricultural land to combine "agriculture and tourism," "agriculture and education," and "agriculture and recreation." The development of leisure agriculture has increased the efficiency of the means of production, increased employment opportunities and boosted the local economy. It is a new measure in the form of a leisure service industry that helps farmers improve their operations.

The Puli Agricultural Association also introduced the activity to set up a combination agricultural and fishing park for each village. In addition to putting on traditional singing performances, exhibitions, ecological forest tourism, and nature conservation activities, the association also set up a special bus service to take tourists from one site in the park to another so the tourists can conveniently see the entire park and allow individual tourists to visit and enjoy sites operated jointly by local residents and buy local produce. In addition, the Puli Agricultural Association is strongly promoting the formation of an alliance with the Tienshulien Hotel, Puli Distillery and the Taiyi Ecological, Educational and Leisure Agricultural Park in a powerful effort to develop the leisure and education functions of traditional agriculture.

The leisure agriculture of Puli has improved the competitiveness of the local agriculture and created a green miracle in the Taiwan region. Encouraging farmers to make use of the special local agricultural scenery and rural culture, and allowing tourists to truly appreciate rural life has not only changed the traditional structure of

Small frog-shaped
wooden building

agriculture, but also boosted local economic development
and growth and greatly helped overall social development. Leisure agriculture has increased the sources of income for local farmers and made corresponding improvements in their standard of living.

A prime example of Puli leisure agriculture is the Taiyi
Ecological, Educational and Leisure Agricultural Park.
The 10-hectare park is located in the Puli Basin in Nantou
County, with its clear mountain water and mild climate.
The park makes use of Puli's ample agricultural resources
and human environment to carry out its main purpose of
supplying local farmers with seedlings for growing fruits
and vegetables as well as its secondary activity of developing agricultural tourism and resources for expanding
application of science and technology in agriculture. Entering the park today you can see plots of seedlings and
flowers in a wide variety of colors, offering a spectacular
sight. Inside the park there is a pressed flower center,
which displays beautiful pressed flower articles as well
as provides an opportunity for visitors to make their own
pressed flowers. The education section of the park helps
visitors understand the growth process of plants and provides them with the opportunity to work on a vegetable
plot themselves and better appreciate a farmer's life. Efforts are made to ensure that the ecological environment is

← Flowers growing in
the crevice left by
the September 21
earthquake, where a
temple to the flower
goddess has been built.

kept as pristine as possible and all development projects are required to disturb the ecology of the area as little as possible. Mainly local crops are grown in line with the decision for the park to concentrate on green cultivation. Growing a wide variety of local crops is not only a special feature of the park, it also constitutes a smorgasbord of local crops. Also on display in the park are agricultural tools and equipment such as water carts and windmills to help visitors appreciate rural life and culture.

The rich variety of plants and moving scenes of life on the farm provide visitors with an unforgettable ecological education experience. The park also gives visitors the chance to experience a totally restful stay in one of the park's lodgings—the Fairy Tale Wooden Cabins, which are sloped-roof buildings with exquisite rooms. The Fairy Tale Wooden Cabins are also known as the Earthquake Memorial Cabins. After the September 21, 1999 earthquake, the likes of which only occur once in a century, the people were afraid to sleep in their homes whether they were severely injured or not. Puli was covered with tents then, and these 12 wooden cabins were built later in the shape of tents to commemorate that time.

Fishing Tourism on Changdao Island

Changdao Island, which is under the domain of China, is known as the Miao island chain (called Shamen Island in ancient times), but is called Changdao Island for short. Changdao Island is located between the peninsula of Shandong and eastern Liaoning where the Yellow and Bohai seas meet. It is Shandong's only island county and consists of 32 islands covering 56 square kilometers. The islands have a total coastline of 146 kilometers and a standing population of 45,000. When the Qin Emperor Qinshihuang and Han Emperor Wudi went looking for a spirit to obtain eternal life on the island, the island has been known as a "mountain of the spirits of the sea and a scene of the spirits on earth." Changdao Island features mountains, the sea, islands, reefs, caves and historical sites and is a combination of exotic, elegant, dangerous, sacred, and enchanted things.

Fishing boats and windmills

In summer with intense heat, the island offers a tranquil environment and a cool weather. It is an excellent place to come for tourism, holiday trips, fishing, painting pictures, and adventure; it is a fairyland where visitors spend summer vacations, enjoy cool weather, appreciate novel sights and explore mysteries. The State Council has named Changdao Island as a national-level prime scenic area, national-level protected zone, national-level forest park, and in 2006, as one of the "ten most beautiful islands of China." It is one of the most famous tourist and holiday destinations in China.

Changdao Island is one of the great paradises of China and is the scene of four famous myths and folk legends, "Mazu Protects the Sea," "Eight Immortals Cross the Sea," "Zhang Yu Boils the Sea," and "Jingwei Fills the Sea." The launch of the fishing tourism program allows visitors to come and enjoy a hundred kinds of seafood, sleep on a local fishing family's *kang*, enjoy the natural coastal scenery, purchase local products and learn to appreciate the local customs.

Changdao Island is rich in seafood resources and is known as "the home of abalone, scallops, and kelp in China." In the spring of 1999 the Changdao Island county government introduced the activity called, "Eat in the home of a fishing family, stay in the home of a fishing family, enjoy the life of a fishing family." A number of fishing households were selected that had the proper conditions for receiving guests and their services were publicized to promote tourist groups to come to Changdao Island and stay in their homes on a market-driven basis. The villagers are responsible for specific advertising and promotion activities, transportation arrangements and providing food and lodging, but participating households must strictly comply with the general requirements for the fishing tourism program and provide a full range of services, including food, lodging, transportation, tours, shopping and entertainment. Hard work and constant improvement has resulted in a more and more diverse range of services and activities and the

Beach on Changdao
Island

program is now fairly well developed.

One of the major activities in the fishing tourism program is the "Be a Fisherman for a Day" activity, which allows tourists to personally experience what it's like to work as a fisherman. During the day tourists go out on the fishing boats and cast nets, set traps, and catch crab under the direction of fishermen. The "Tour around the Islands" activity provides tourists with a day of beautiful sights to enjoy. The "Fishing on Diaoyu Island" activity allows visitors to try their hand at fishing on a boat and with fishing equipment provided by the host family. In addition, visitors can enjoy a sea tour of Wanniao Island or make arrangements to take a trip to other nearby tourist attractions.

There is no set menu for meals in the homes of the fishing families and guests can select dishes according to their own preferences. There are usually 8 dishes, including fish, shrimp or crab, shellfish, meat and vegetables, prepared according to local custom. The host may also prepare seaweed dumplings, an island specialty, for their guests accompanied by fish sauce, shrimp sauce, sea monster sauce, sea hare sauce and other flavors of the sea,

Fisherman's hut

Aquafarm raising scallops and sea cucumbers

and guests who are interested may share a few drinks with their hosts.

After dinner guests may watch television, sing Karaoke, play music videos of Changdao Island songs performed by famous stars or simply sit on a folding stool (favorite type of chair for relaxing among fishing families) and shoot the breeze with their hosts. Every evening around 7 PM the villagers stage a folk performance, with a lion dance parading down the street, a bonfire and singing and dancing, in which guests are invited to participate.

Guests may visit any house in the village, take strolls down the streets, collect shells along the shore outside the village or go up on the hill behind Wanggou Village to see the famous "ancestor tree," said to have been brought here from Yunnan by people when they immigrated here.

The Changdao Island people have carefully created two new items in its fishing tourism program, the "Comfortable Fishing Home" and "Sea Tour with a Fisherman" activities. The blue sky, azul sea, ample sunlight, sea beaches and pure seaside air plus the local people with their simple, enthusiastic and straightforward personality combine to make Changdao Island an eco-friendly, safe and healthy tourist destination.

Turpan Grape Valley

Grape Valley is located in Grape Township of the city of Turpan, about 15 kilometers northeast of the central city district of Turpan and is a valley in the western section of Huoyan (flame) Mountain known for grape cultivation.

Grape Valley is about 8 kilometers in length from north to south and 0.6 to 2 kilometers wide from east to west with a narrow shape and smooth terrain. Steep cliffs rise on either side of the valley like protective screens.

Seedless green grapes

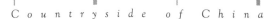

A stream carrying good-quality water flows through the valley. Grape trellises have been erected on both sides of the stream and they are covered with grapes. The surrounding area is thickly covered with white poplars interspersed with grass, flowers and fruit trees that the local residents have carefully planted in rows on the gentle slopes.

Walking into Grape Valley is like walking into a cool new world. Nearly a hundred grape vines the thickness of a bowl are on the cement grape trellises, which are densely covered in leaves and bunches of glittering grapes.

The people of Xinjiang say, "People praise the grapes of Turpan, the musk melons of Hami, and the fragrant

Bird's-eye view of Grape Valley, Turpan

Muscat grapes

as "Bujluq," meaning a land where grapes are numerous and fine in quality. There are 13 main varieties grown here, including seedless green grapes, red grapes, and Kashmir grapes. The shape of the grapes includes round, egg-shaped and oval varieties. Some are sparkling like pearls, some are brightly colored like agate, and some are green like jade. Grape Valley thus resembles a grape museum. Of particular note are the seedless green grapes, which have thin skins and tender flesh. They are juicy, delicious, and nutritious, causing people to compare them to pearls. They have a sugar content of 20–24%, surpassing that of California grapes and becoming highest in the world. Raisins made from the seedless grapes can have a sugar content of over 60%, making them tart, sweet, and delicious. They have a high reputation on the international market and are known as "green pearls of China."

In the central part of Grape Valley below the east cliff wall is a grape orchard covering over 50 *mu* in area. This is a major Turpan tourist attraction for domestic and overseas guests opened in 1982 following the government's

Endless varieties of grapes for you to taste

seas guests opened in 1982 following the government's institution of the reform and opening up policy. The orchard contains small bridges and flowing water, ancient towering trees, cool sweet fountains, ponds of limpid water, row after row of grape trellises forming green corridors, wide and tranquil green paths, clean and elegant restaurants and myriads of small stalls selling carefully made handicrafts and tourist souvenirs. The many bunches of ripe grapes within arm's reach are sparkling, transparent and fragrant. When the Uygurs perform their traditional dance under the grape trellises, young Uyghur girls enthusiastically invite guests to participate and join the fun. Friendly hosts pick bunches of fresh grapes for visitors to taste.

Snow melt from Tianshan Mountains has been directed to flow through the valley and the sound of the trickling water through Grape Valley gives it a special spirit and at the same time waters the terraced fields on the two sides of the valley. Anyone who comes to Turpan and doesn't try the sweet refreshing grapes of Grape Valley will never appreciate the cool side of the scorching Turpan Basin.

Tengtou Village of Fenghua, Zhejiang

Tengtou Village is located in the northern part of the city of Fenghua, Zhejiang Province, about 6 kilometers from the central city district in the plains under the jurisdiction of the town of Xiaowangmiao. According to the Qing Dynasty *Records of Fenghua County* (*Emperor Guangxu*), 90% of the population were surnamed Fu. The village is located in a vast open plain and is neat and clean, has good transportation facilities and a population that is simple and honest. The village was listed to the 1992 "Global 500" for environmental protection by the United Nations Environment Program. In 1997 it was named as a "National Environmental Education Base."

These beautiful surroundings attract many urban tourists.

Longstreet Banquet at the start of the fiesta in Tengtou Village. A thousand people dined at tables 100 meters long, feasting on a variety of grains such as sorghum, rye, millet, corn and rice and local snacks like steamed rice bread, yellow glutinous rice cakes, maci, New Year's cake, preserved winter melon and roasted vegetables.

Tengtou Village was formerly known as "Destitute Tengtou" because of the poor conditions in the village. The surrounding rivers were narrow and the scattering of agricultural plots in the village were subject to yearly flooding. There were over 80 households with 401 people living in the village in 1949, mainly living off rice paddies. Out of the nearly 1,000 *mu* of farmland, 60% was held by absentee landlords, leaving only 300 *mu* (including that of clans) for the local residents.

Tourists pick strawberries in a greenhouse.

In the 1960s and 1970s the people of Tengtou adopted an attitude of "nose to the plow" and used their "carrying poles and shoulders" to convert the more than 1,200 plots of low-yield land of varying altitudes and sizes that were subject to yearly flooding into more than 200 good plots. The new well-drained plots are all the same size and lined up in a north-south orientation thereby greatly improving the quality and size of harvests.

In the 1980s the people of Tengtou began working very

South African agriculture officials learn to pollinate vegetables in a greenhouse.

hard and making many sacrifices to develop local industry from one garment factory employing 27 people to 37 enterprises in four industrial zones today. The Tengtou Group has an annual production output worth one billion yuan, making it the rural enterprise with the largest scale of operations and greatest total of tax and profits in China.

As the people of Tengtou gradually began to prosper in the mid-1990s they stepped up their self-improvement efforts and began attaching more importance to the concept of sustainable development. Tengtou was named as a national-level model eco-friendly village and reached its goals for modernization of agriculture and the countryside ahead of schedule.

In addition to working to improve their material standard of living, the people of Tengtou also stepped up efforts to improve spiritual civilization, creating a village of simple and honest people with an excellent social atmo-

97

sphere of unity and harmony among neighbors.

To improve living conditions, the simple utilitarian farm houses were demolished and all replaced with deluxe modern houses with so that all the villagers could live in spacious and comfortable conditions, increasing the per capital housing of 40 square meters to 80 square meters. The village also provides welfare benefits such as medical insurance and old-age insurance for all its residents. There is not one economically deprived household in the village. All are living a comfortable life.

While continuing to develop the tourist industry, Tengtou Village is also developing and making use of new scenic spots while ensuring that buildings in the village fit in well with the natural environment. The pastoral scenery is exquisite and the environment is very suitable for human habitation. Eco-tours cover dozens of scenic sites, including Jiangnan Park, General Forest, Potted Landscape Park and Green Corridor. For tourists interested in agriculture there is the Plant Cultivation Sightseeing Park, the Flower, Grass and Tree Appreciation Zone and the Seed and Seedling Cultivation Base and Seasonal Fruit and Melon Patch, where visitors can pick their own fruit and melons. Tourists interested in the local customs and traditions can participate in activities such as spinning and weaving, crossing the fields on footpaths between plots, drawing water with a water wheel, and hulling the spring rice and see trail blazing animal performances such as bull fighting, goat fighting, pig races and cock fighting. The overall effect is a beautiful picture of human and nature in harmony. Tengtou Village pursues a civilized development path of working to expand production, increase standard of living and maintain an excellent ecological environment while maintaining a balance among rapid economic development, environmental concerns and the building of spiritual civilization. The village has become a model exemplar of the eco-friendly, modern, new socialist countryside.

Guangxi Buluotuo Scenic Mango Orchard

The Guangxi Buluotuo Scenic Mango Orchard is located in Baiyu Village in Baiyu Town of Tianyang County, about 5 kilometers from the city district of the county. National highway Route 324 runs by the entrance to the scenic area and the Nanning-Kunming Railway passes along the area, so transportation is never a problem. The main theme of the scenic area is the mangoes, but the rural sightseeing tour combines mango production, application of modern agricultural techniques, rural sightseeing and rest and recreation. The orchard

Tourists sample mangos in the mango orchard.

helps increase scientific knowledge among the masses, raises the incomes of the local people as well as meets a wide range of consumer demands. In July 2005, the orchard was named as a national model for agricultural tourism and was approved as an autonomous zone.

Captivating Tianyang mangos

In 1985 Tianyang County made the strategic decision to set up the Youjiang Valley Mango Product Production Base and concentrate on development of mango production as a key industry in reviving the economy of Tianyang County and helping the local people throw off poverty. The local government formulated a development plan for linking plots together, introduced favorable policies and developed a policy of relying on a combination state, collective and private ownership to strongly promote development of mango production. The scenic orchard greatly benefits from government direction and the bootstrap effect of state and collective participation in encouraging all local farmers to develop mango production. Mango cultivation has now reached 130,000 *mu* in Tianyang County. Increasing farmer incomes and mango production has become a way for local residents

Happily harvesting

to throw off poverty and begin living better lives. In 1995 Tianyang County became the largest mango producing county in the country, and in April of that year the Ministry of Agriculture named the county "China's Mango Village." A mango variety produced in the county won silver medal (highest award that year) in its category at the First China Agricultural Exhibition held in 1992 and gold medal at the second   held in 1995, and was called,   "king of

The main building of
Jinsui Orchard

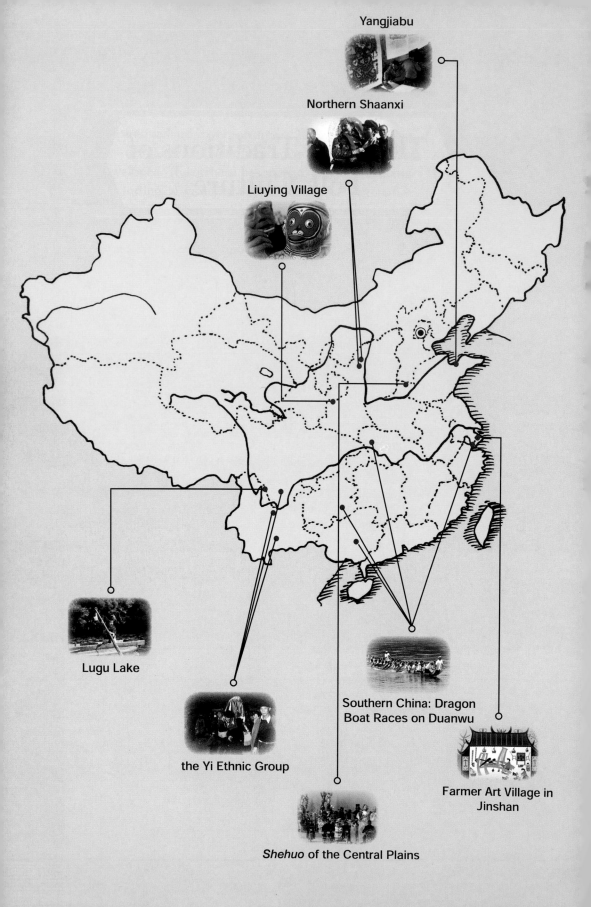

Yangjiabu

Northern Shaanxi

Liuying Village

Lugu Lake

the Yi Ethnic Group

Southern China: Dragon Boat Races on Duanwu

Farmer Art Village in Jinshan

Shehuo of the Central Plains

Lugu Lake: Exotic Oriental Land of Women

Lugu Lake, 200 kilometers from the city center of Lijiang, Yunnan, resembles a sparkling jewel nestled in the high plateau among the many mountains of western Yunnan. Living among the unsurpassed beauty of the lake and mountains live the Mosuo people, one of the few peoples in the world still living in a matriarchal society. Their unique *"azhu"* marriage ceremony and natural and primitive folk customs have given this ancient land an air of mystery and romance, and for this reason it is known as the "exotic oriental land of daughters."

An ancient local legend explains the origin of Lugu Lake as follows. Gemu, the female spirit, was a wise and

Surface of the lake and Lige Peninsula

beautiful young woman who was not only the girlfriend of many local male mountain spirits, but of distant male mountain spirits as well. One time when a distant male mountain spirit came to visit her she was having a rendezvous with a local male mountain spirit. He hurriedly turned the horse around, causing it to neigh three times. When she heard the sound of the horse she immediately chased after the visiting mountain spirit, but he was already far away and all she could see was a large hoof print at the bottom of the mountain. By the time she reached the hoof print, the sun was coming up and she stood by the hoof print sobbing uncontrollably until her tears filled the hoof print, forming the present Lugu Lake. When the departing mountain spirit heard the sound of her sobbing he turned around to look and lovingly threw some pearls and flowers into the lake. The pearls became small islands in the lake and the flowers floated to the shore and grew into a fragrant patch of flowers, including azaleas, which bloom year after year.

In actuality, Lugu Lake was formed by a fault in the earth. It has an area of 50 square kilometers and averages about 45 meters in depth. The lake is shaped like a horse hoof, long north-south and short east-west in the shape of a gourd. The scenery around the lake changes constantly during the day as the surrounding mountains fade in and out of view. The undulating shoreline creates many

Outlet of Lugu Lake—Caohai, located in Yanyuan County, Sichuan

Houses along the lake

beaches, some large, some small, on the long shore of the lake, making it a perfect spot for tourists to relax and play.

The last matriarchal society in the world is found by Lugu Lake. In the *"azhu* marriage" of the Mosuo, the man does not marry the woman and vice-versa. In work, life and financial matters, the couple does not have to remain in contact. *"azhu"* is a word in the Mosuo language that means "intimate sweetheart." An *"uzhu"* marriage is based on feeling and each partner is free to come and go as they wish. Mosuo marriages come in three forms:

Azhu marriage without cohabitation

In an *azhu* marriage without cohabitation, the man does not marry the woman and vice-versa. The man and woman both continue to live in their parents' home. The

man only goes to the woman's home to spend the night and then returns to his mother's home in the morning to work and live. This is known as a "traveling marriage." Children resulting from an *azhu* marriage without cohabitation are considered members of the woman's family, take the woman's last name and are raised in her mother's home. Though the father does not live together with his children, he often visits them and stays interested in their lives and development. The father may send gifts of clothing and daily necessities and children may visit the father's home on holidays.

Azhu marriage with cohabitation

In an *azhu* marriage with cohabitation, as opposed to the *azhu* marriage without cohabitation, the married couple does not live apart with their individual parents. Instead, they live, work, and raise their children together in either his or her parents' home, making it unnecessary for the man to visit his wife at night and leave again the next morning. This kind of marriage takes form when a

Mosuo girl rowing a boat

Life beside the lake

couple has been living in a "traveling" marriage for some time and discovered that they have deep feelings for each other and both wish to solidify their relationship as they approach middle age or their parents have died, releasing their obligation to care for them. If the couple discover they no longer care for each other after they have lived together for a period of time they can choose to separate and each live in their mother's home. Because the couple are living together rather than having their own separate homes, planning their own separate lives and working apart from each other, the property belongs to the family in whose home the couple lives. Regardless of whether the man or woman later leaves, all property stays with the family, as do any children. After the couple split, each has an economic safety net to fall back on in the form of their families and later problems are avoided since neither has to worry about how they are going to live.

One-on-one marriage

Among the Mosuo, 20% practice one-on-one marriage. After Kublai Khan led the Mongolian Army south to Lugu Lake, he set up a feudal government system, installed warrant officers and stationed troops there. He also introduced Lamaism and exercised a rule that combined civil administration and religion in Yongning and Lugu Lake. The new officials continued to practice their traditional monogamous marriage. Mosuo people living in Jiaze and Tuodian and sites near the county seat such as Yankouba and Wakai have also been gradually adopting the practice of one-on-one marriage after a long time living among other ethnic groups. Some Mosuo, however, have retained the custom of showing greatest respect for mothers and parents-in-law, with mothers enjoying especially high social status.

Forced Marriage of the Yi Ethnic Group

The bride's family carefully dresses the bride with new felt and silver decorations.

The Yi ethnic group is one of the larger ethnic minority groups of the more than 50 recognized groups in China, and its population is widely dispersed, with the greatest concentrations in Liangshan of Sichuan and Chuxiong and Honghe of Yunnan. Because there are many branches of Yi and they are widely dispersed, there are differences in the marriage customs, which tend to be more like those of the local population. In general though, they all go through the same process: first become friends, then consult a matchmaker, followed by pre-engagement, getting engaged, the man takes a wife and the couple get married.

Girls from the bride's family use soot to blacken the faces of a representative of the groom.

Yi people generally wait until at least until the age of 17 before getting married. At the time they marry, the groom's age must be even and the bride's odd. Most couples choose to marry during the fall and winter slack time for agriculture after the grain has been stored in the silos, the lambs have been slaughtered and the wild geese have flown south or during the Chinese New Year celebrations. Before the wedding ceremony, the bride is not allowed to eat anything for one, two or more days, and the day before may not drink any water to ensure that she will not have to stop to relieve herself on the way to the house of his future parents-in-law. Before the groom can marry the bride, her family must send two young men, known as "xiamu" (usually cousins of the groom) to present liquor to the groom's family to indicate the wedding ceremony will take place as scheduled. When the bride goes to the groom's village, he does not go directly to the bride's house. Instead he goes to the hut he has constructed for the purpose ahead of time made of new bamboo, pine branches and bamboo screens, known as the "Relative Reception Hut." The bamboo and pine branches signify that the bride and groom will

Before daybreak, representatives of the groom leave with the bride they have captured.

always feel as young as the bamboo and pine and live together until they are old and gray. People twine blue and white strips of cloth into the bride's hair before she enters the home of the groom's family at night (signaled by the stars coming out) and then bury the cloth under a peach or pear tree. After the bride enters the home of the husband's family, she eats her first meal since the beginning of her fast, the "crossing the threshold meal," accompanied by the sisters of the groom. At this time the groom cannot show his face and cannot even turn on the light while the others are eating. The next day (same day in some areas) the bride returns home along with the relatives that accompanied her. The second day after the bride goes back home, the groom pays a return visit to her family accompanied by some young people of the village carrying alcoholic beverages and meat and leading a sheep and a pig. After a few more days the groom's family sends people to greet the bride and the new couple begin their life together as husband and wife.

The Yi ethnic group believe that fresh water can get

At the wedding, girls dance
felt dance.

At the wedding banquet,
guests freely drink fine wine.

rid of evil, exorcize ghosts and bring good luck. The bride must therefore be splashed with water. The man's family selects several unmarried young men of the family who are strong and capable, able to ward off the cold water splashed by the villagers and able to carry out the difficult task of "kidnapping the bride." Actually, both bride and groom are willing participants in the so-called kidnapping of the bride, and the parents agree with it and the intermediary arranges it since it is just a marriage custom. The young men sent by the man's family give gifts to the woman's family while rolling up the bride in a carpet. People in the woman's family pretend like they are trying to fight off the "kidnappers" and put soot from the bottom of a pot on the faces of the couple. In southern Yunnan, the time and place of the kidnapping are all pre-arranged, often while the woman is in the fields working or returning home after collecting firewood or collecting straw on the outskirts of the village. The captured woman is led directly to the living room of the man's family. In accordance with local Li custom, once the woman reaches the living room of the man's family she is considered formally married and cannot run away.

Northern Shaanxi: Simple Yet Precise Village Marriage Ceremony

Northern Shaanxi boys are called lads and girls are called daughters before they marry and called man and wife afterwards. When a girl reaches the age of 17 or 18 her family finds someone for her (called a boyfriend). They don't place much importance on how much money the family has or how much property they own, concentrating more on whether or not the potential boyfriend is sincere and truly ready to make progress. The meeting of the girl and boy is fairly simple and the couple only makes sure they are compatible, placing more emphasis on

Elderly man gaily leads mule decorated with red cloth.

Boisterous music on the road

whether or not they can live together happily rather than how well they can carry out house chores.

The engagement ceremony takes place in the man's home. The ceremony is fairly simple. The woman's family sends a senior member of the family, usually the bride's father, to go with the bride and participate in the ceremony. The man's family does not put on a grand affair. They only invite a few close relatives, such as aunts, uncles and sisters of the groom, plus a few good friends of the groom to participate. After the two sides greet each other, they sit down for a noon banquet, the groom's family present gifts to the bride's family and the ceremony is considered finished.

Marriages in northern Shaanxi usually take place in the winter, when the year's farm work is over and people have more spare time. In some other areas where transportation is difficult and economic conditions are poor, vegetables, meat, fish and fowl do not spoil easily and

The wedding formally begins in the space in front of a cave dwelling.

Villagers along the way come out to watch the commotion.

Arriving at the groom's home, the groom carries the bride into the cave dwelling.

can be kept for a long time.

The marriage ceremony takes three days to complete and is divided into two parts, the process of the girl leaving home to get married and the boy going to pick up his new bride. The length of the marriage ceremony is determined by a certain number of meals, usually four.

Before the marriage ceremony, the man's family goes to the home of the woman to talk to the head of her family and formally request her hand in marriage. Sometimes the woman's family may invite the man's family to come and ask for the marriage, usually because the woman is old enough. To avoid the occurrence of any problems, they invite the man to take the woman away to marry her. After the two parties come to an agreement, the man goes home to select an auspicious date and make preparations before formally marrying the woman. Two days before the selected date for the ceremony, the woman begins the process of leaving home to get married. On this

day the woman leaves her home to live in someone else's home fairly far away from her own and cannot return or receive food from home. This is called "leaving the house," meaning leaving her family's home. In the evening a relative of the groom comes to give her clothing, ornaments and some daily necessities. On the second day the bride puts on the clothing and ornaments, and gets dressed from head to foot in preparation for the groom's representatives to come for her.

The man's family usually sends 4 to 6 members as representatives to pick up the bride. An older relative of the groom, usually an uncle, represents the groom's family in communicating with the bride's family and handling financial matters and miscellaneous tasks. One is the advance party, usually an uncle of the groom, who is responsible for communicating the good news to the groom's family. Sometimes the groom's family will send a band to serenade the bride. The marriage scene is very lively, with blaring suonas, exploding fireworks and many happy faces as the representatives of the groom distribute candy and cigarettes to the guests.

Before transportation conditions improved, the groom would lead a mule ridden by the bride while everyone else walked. Later it was changed to four representatives of the groom carrying the bride in a sedan chair. With improved economic conditions, the bride is usually picked up in a well-decorated automobile, and the car used has become more and more upscale.

Southern China: Dragon Boat Races on Duanwu

The dragon boat races are the main feature of the Duanwu Festival of southern China (the 5th day of the 5th lunar month), which is said to have begun in the Spring and Autumn Period and the period of the Warring States. During this period the worthy official Qu Yuan (340–278 BC) of the State of Chu jumped into a river, and his countrymen vied to save him, but he disappeared in Dongting Lake without a trace. Every year after this on the 5th day of the 5th lunar month people rowed boats on the river to scatter the fish and keep them from eating Qu Yuan's body. The custom then spread throughout the states of Wu, Yue, and Chu.

There is another version of how the dragon boat races began. In primitive totem society, people worshipped the image of the powerful dragon as their own ancestor and protective spirit (as a totem). Tribal people who lived in

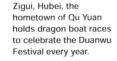

Zigui, Hubei, the hometown of Qu Yuan holds dragon boat races to celebrate the Duanwu Festival every year.

regions of lakes and rivers built boats in the shape of a dragon and decorated them with illustrations of dragons to protect them from the harm of snakes, insects, disease, and the threat of floods. Every year during the Duanwu Festival they hold the dragon race to show their reverence for the dragon and to show that they are descendants of the dragon.

Annual dragon boat race of a village in Quangang District, Quanzhou, Fujian

The dragon boat races, in addition to being a way to remember Qu Yuan, are given other implications in other areas. In Guangxi they are known as "pushing dragon boats" and are a favorite mass sport among the local people. In Jiangsu and Zhejiang area, the dragon boat races are also held in honor of Qiu Jin, a locally born modern revolutionary. The sight at night on the dragon boats is a moving and exciting one, with the colorful lanterns on boats and the boats weaving in and out and up and down the river. The Miao people of Guizhou hold a "Dragon Boat Festival" from the 25th to the 28th of the 5th month of the lunar calendar to celebrate success in the planting of seedlings and wish for a bountiful grain harvest. The people of different ethnic groups and different areas have different explanations for the dragon boat races. Down to the present many areas in southern China located near rivers, lakes, and seas hold dragon boat races and activities with their own characteristics every year during the Duanwu Festival.

People in Taiwan began holding dragon boat races during the 29th year of the reign of the Qing Dynasty Emperor Qianlong (1739 AD) and they now hold them every year on the 5th day of the 5th lunar month. Dragon boat races are also held in Hong Kong and people in England also hold races after the Chinese custom, organizing teams for the activity. In addition, the custom of holding dragon boat races has spread to neighboring countries such as Japan and Vietnam.

The dragon boat races always attract large numbers of tourists and the two banks of the river are always covered with people cheering, yelling, setting off fireworks and banging gongs. Dragon boat races are held in villages, towns and counties and in some places the races are connected with activities to promote friendship and commercial ties. In order to better develop this traditional festival custom, the State Physical Culture administration organized and set up the Dragon Boat Association and declared an annual National Dragon Boat Month be ob-

Annual dragon boat race held by Dong people living on the Liujiang River in Sandu County, Guizhou

served every year. The organization and leadership of the Dragon Boat Association covers the dragon boat competitions in China and abroad and both competition and traditional dragon boats to ensure that Dragon Boat Month is a brilliant success. The scope of dragon boat races has continued to grow, expanding from southern China to northern China and from rural residents to college students.

Dragon boat race during the Water-Sprinkling Festival the Dai ethnic group from Xishuangbanna, Yunnan Province

Shehuo of the Central Plains

*S*hehuo of the Central Plains is an activity staged by the local people for their own entertainment during the Chinese New Year period. It originated from the ancient reverence for earth and fire. *She* stands for the spirit of the earth and *huo* stands for the fire ancestor, said to be a fire spirit that could ward off difficulties and evil. In a country like China, noted for its agricultural culture, the earth is the material base for the people's survival and development. Fire is the source of heat for cooking food and keeping warm and is also absolutely essential for the survival and development of humankind. According to the primitive theories of people in the ancient past, people believed that fire contained a special kind of spirit, which they began to worship because of the great value they placed on it. This worship of earth and fire among the ancient

Performance of Bei'ge dance in Xunxian County, Henan

Dazzling performance of Taizhuang dance by farmers in Songxian, Henan

people of the Central Plains led to holding ceremonies to honor them. As society changed and evolved, *Shehuo* has become a large-scale mass cultural activity for celebrating the holiday in many areas and an entertainment activity for the masses in anticipation of good weather, a bumper grain harvest and national peace and stability.

The folk custom of *Shehuo* of the Central Plains has a long history. In and around Xunxian County of Henan

In addition to the Central Plains, Shehuo performances are also popular in the rural northwest. Photo: Performance on stilts at Ta'er Temple, Qinghai.

the custom can be traced back to the 4th century AD during the Eastern Jin and Later Zhao periods of Chinese history. It continued to develop through the Tang and Song dynasties and matured in the Ming and Qing period. *Shehuo*, as a kind of traditional mass entertainment activity, has enriched the cultural life of the people and effectively boosted the development of folk culture and folk customs.

Around the time of the Chinese New Year is peak season for this traditional entertainment activity in the areas of the Central Plains inhabited by Han Chinese. Particularly after the Chinese New Year from the 10th to the 15th of the first lunar month when people have completed the traditional round of visits to relatives, the people of villages throughout the area have spare time to engage in *Shehuo*.

During this time the village divides into several groups, and groups may be formed with members of other villages. Funding of the activity comes from voluntary contributions and a person in charge of the *Shehuo* is responsible for managing human resources, material resources and financial resources.

Shehuo activities usually take place in a wide-open space outdoors. Where ever *Shehuo* activities take place, people announce their arrival by lighting strings of firecrackers. The activities are usually held on an open-air stage and people come from all over the local area to participate.

Shehuo gets off to a grand start, accompanied by firecrackers, gongs, and drums. The opening act opens up a corridor for the *Shehuo* through the sea of people. The rhythm of the gongs and drums is strong and fast, and the gong and drum band is the soul of *Shehuo*. The drummer of the band is like the conductor for the activities since the drummer is the one who controls the tempo.

The act with the highest degree of difficulty is usually the one in which young girls and boys (usually 4 or 5 years old) dressed in costume stand on the top of a steel rod 2 or 3 meters long or even longer that is fixed to a table. The top of the rod is decorated with colored paper in the form of cotton blossoms, fruit trees, clouds, tigers, or other ferocious animals depending on the content of the skit. This act is at least as dangerous as acrobatics.

Performance of large Qiaoqiaogang in Xunxian County, Henan

Shehuo performance in Yangxian County, Shaanxi, using modern traffic facilities

The decorated truck performance features people dressed as famous figures from the past and present to form a tableau riding on a carefully decorated truck. The clothing, props, and program for the decorated truck performance are prepared and planned in advance by some experienced personnel. Each group of villagers puts on act to show their particular talents.

The content of *Shehuo* in the Central Plains is rich and the forms diverse, including walking on stilts, paddling the land boat, the lion dance, and the lantern dance. Statistics show that there are over 200 forms of this celebration including gongs and drums, folk dancing, cars, boats and sedan chairs, and martial arts.

Traditional Wooden Chinese New Year Pictures of Yangjiabu, Weifang

The art of making Yangjiabu traditional wooden Chinese New Year pictures resembles an exotic flower among the treasures of folk arts in China and is famous in China and overseas for its strong pastoral flavor and simple, fresh artistic style.

The village of Yangjiabu, Weifang is one of the three

Village sign for Yangjiabu

main production centers for traditional wooden Chinese New Year pictures (Yangliuqing in Tianjin, Taohuawu in Suzhou, and Yangjiabu in Hanting). The techniques used in the pictures from Yangjiabu have been developed and improved over the course of hundreds of years in accordance with the ideological requirements, customs and beliefs, aesthetic concepts and daily necessities of the local farmers to create their own ancient, elegant, unrefined, and bright style.

Yangjiabu traditional wooden Chinese New Year pictures have a long history. As long ago as the Ming Dynasty in the village "every house made traditional Chinese New Year Pictures and everyone flew kites." The

New Year's door god pictures in Yangjiabu

"Jixinghao" Chinese New Year Picture Workshop, founded in the 13th year of the reign Ming Emperor Chongzhen (1640), has 239.4 square meters and 11 rooms. The building is well-preserved and under provincial protection. Mass production and sale of the wooden Chinese New Year pictures began and thrived during the reign of the Qing Emperor Qianlong, and Yangjiabu, "the village with a hundred art shops, a thousand different Chinese New Year pictures and tens of thousands of drawing boards," has remained one of the top three regions for the production of the pictures in the century and a half since then.

A diverse array of subjects is depicted in the Yangjiabu traditional wooden Chinese New Year pictures in many different forms and types. The main subjects include wishes for prosperity and good luck, wishes to avoid disasters and calamities, beautiful women and children, wishes for luck and happiness, people's everyday life, men at farming and women at weaving, novels and

traditional operas, myths and legends, natural scenery, and flying birds and stalking animals. Some also feature practical items used in daily life. Yangjiabu traditional wooden Chinese New Year pictures have become part of international cultural exchange attracting foreign business people and tourists and a pivotal area for developing the global-market-oriented economy of Weifang.

As New Year's draws near, everyone busily prints Chinese New Year's pictures.

The Yangjiabu Folk Art Scenic Park is located on the west side of the village of Yangjiabu in the Hanting District of Weifang, Shandong and is a national AAA sightseeing and tourist area. The sightseeing area was set up

Stamps issued by China Post of wooden Chinese New Year's pictures from Yangjiabu

People beat gongs and drums to welcome in the Chinese New Year.

in 1986 with an area of 240 *mu*. The park combines rest and recreation with folk art production, exhibition and participation activities as an important scenic area in the Shandong Thousand-*li* Folk Customs Tour. The park is divided into four exhibition zones for the art of Yangjiabu traditional wooden Chinese New Year pictures, the art of kites, folk culture and art on the Yangjiabu Old Shopping Street and the culture and art of Zheng Banqiao. There are a total of 28 individual sights. Tourists can gain a thorough understanding of the history and the ancient and unique production techniques in use for over 600 years to make the traditional Chinese New Year pictures. Tourists can also watch the whole traditional process for making Yangjiabu kites, enjoy the kite exhibition and enjoy the sight of kites looking like "paper flowers filling the sky like snow flurries." Other folk art attractions include paper cutting, redwood inlaid with silver, clay figures, dough figures, Cloisonné and silver statues. Tour-

ists can also gain an appreciation for the heart and soul of the culture of Zheng Banqiao. Visitors from far and wide are attracted to the ancient Ming Dynasty scholar trees, the special style of the Ming and Qing dynasty buildings, the tranquil rural courtyard houses with their imposing gate spirits and great inner screen walls depicting luck, prosperity and long life, and the ancient and simple folk customs of the local people.

The Yangjiabu Folk Art Scenic Park is a gallery for folk art and a great place for domestic and foreign tourists to come to appreciate folk art. Reactions from visitors have been very good. The scenic area has been named as a "National Model for Agricultural Tourism," one of the "56 Scenic Areas in the Country with the Most Ethnic Flavor," one of the "Top Ten Brands in Tourism and Recreation Sites in Shandong" and "Model in Shandong Agricultural Tourism." The Chinese New Year pictures and kites of Yangjiabu have been recognized as a "Famous Shandong Trademark" brand.

Farmer Art Village in Jinshan District, Shanghai

The Jinshan Farmer Art Village Ecological and Recreation Park is located in Zhonghong Village in Fengjing Town in the Jinshan District of Shanghai. The north side of the village borders on Liantang, Qingpu, the east side adjoins Xinbang, Songjiang and the west side abuts Jiashan, Zhejiang. It is an incorporated village in the "Chinese town famous for its history and culture," Fengjing.

Zhonghong is the original home of Jinshan farmer art. In the 1960s farmers in the Jinshan area began to place more importance on their own aesthetic values, rejecting the traditional creation methods of art academies, and began to concentrate on the creation of art. They began to devote

Zhonghong Village, a farmer art village in Jinshan

An artist in the process of making a farmer painting

themselves to their art leading to the blossoming of this exotic flower of folk art—Jinshan farmer art. A group of farmers from this village combined ancient techniques, such as printing and dyeing, needlework, wood carving and kitchen murals, to create pictures with subjects chosen from a wide range of customs and work activities of rural southern China. They use simple techniques to create many farmer paintings with strong rural flavor. The "Shanghai Jinshan Farmer Art Exhibition" opened in Beijing in 1980 at the Beijing China Art Museum and took Beijing by storm. That same year Jinshan farmer art went global and was exhibited in dozens of countries and regions. As its fame spread around the world, it became known as "China's finest folk art form." In 2000 the National United Folk Art Exhibition was held in Fengjing and was an unprecedented success. In February 2006 Jinshan farmer art was called "an essential feature of China." That same year Zhonghong was named as a "special Chinese village" by the Association for the Promotion of Chinese Village Society thanks to the strength of the local economy and the brilliance of its folk art.

The total planned area of the Jinshan Farmer Art Village and Ecological Recreation Park is 4,500 *mu* and is divided into five scenic areas, called the "Danqing Area," the "Fengjing Area," the "Water House," the "Vegetable Patch Area" and the "Rice Area." The completed "Danqing Area" covers an area of 100 *mu* and is at the heart of the Fengjing Ecological Recreation Park. This is fertile ground for art and a playground for creation, as well as a "Shangri-La" where visitors can rest and play to their hearts' content. In the Jinshan Farmer Art Village visitors can see first hand the entire process of creation and execution of farmer art made by the famous farmer artists of Zhonghong, enjoy the finest works of Jinshan farmer art and purchase certified farmer art originals.

The people of Jinshan Farmer Art Village are simple and the scenery is picturesque. Typical pastoral elements such as small bridges, running water, irrigation water-wheels, grass shacks, vegetable patches, fish ponds and threshing floors add to the pastoral atmosphere of the village. Visitors to the village can observe farmer artists at work and try creating art for themselves as well as view some outstanding examples of farmer art in the exhibition center. Here visitors can also sample authentic original country cuisine and purchase fresh seasonal agricultural products as well as experience first hand the creaking

Bride weaving – a farmer painting

water wheel, the thatched cottages with bamboo fences, the vegetable patches and fish ponds, and the orchards of fruit trees and bamboo.

In the ancient town of Fengjing, the residents all have many farmer paintings on their walls.

The Jinshan Farmer Art Village is a new center for the creation of farmer art and a new stage for the exhibition of farmer art. It is also a new bright spot in countryside tourism in China and a place that demonstrates the new style of the Chinese farmer in the new century.

Museum of Jinshan farmer paintings in Fengjing

Home of Plaster Statues—Liuying (Camp Six) Village in Fengxiang, Shaanxi

engxiang County in Shaanxi is the nationally famous home of plaster statuary. Fengxiang has a long history of making painted plaster statuary. That history began in the Western Zhou Dynasty before the founding of the Qin Dynasty and has been passed down among the people for three thousand years to become China's most ancient and most characteristic handmade plaster statue art. The main producing area for painted plaster statuary today is Liuying (Camp Six) Village, which still carries the name of an ancient military unit.

Legend has it that during the time of transition between the Yuan and Ming dynasties, the Camp Six army unit of Zhu Yuanzhang (1328–1398, founder of the Ming

Clay sculptor Hu Shen from Liuying Village with his sculptures

In the process of making a clay monkey

Dynasty) was stationed in the area of today's Liuying Village in Fengxiang County. Many of the soldiers, most of whom came from Jingdezhen, Jiangxi, famous for its porcelain, later settled in Liuying. They were all skilled in making handmade pottery, and during the slack agricultural season made toys and gift items for sale. Over time, this folk art spread, until Liuying Village became known near and far as "Plaster Statue Village."

The plaster statues of Liuying Village use the unique local white clay as the base and are formed using traditional manual techniques. The statues are then painted in highly contrasting colors, mainly red, green and black. They come in a variety of forms, mainly birds, insects, fish and auspicious fowl and wild animals, strongly reflecting the wishes of the local people for peace and prosperity. The art of Liuying plaster statues infiltrated

In winter, a villager sits shrouded by a quilt making clay figures.

the culture of auspiciousness of rural northern China and mainly reflects their desire for a good life, prosperity and their wishes to avoid disaster and court good luck as the main themes. In addition to this, their skillful combination of simplicity and refinement has won them a place in the art market.

The plaster statues were formerly folk art pieces made by the local villagers during the slack agricultural season and it gave them something interesting to do during this normally uninteresting time. They put their work in a handcart and went from village to village to sell them and supplement their meager incomes. Today many villagers have made plaster statuary production their main occupation and are prospering from it. Entering Liuying Village, one can see partially finished plaster statues everywhere through many the open courtyard doors. About 80 of the 480 households of the village are engaged in making statues, producing a total of 350,000 pieces per year to meet orders of 1 million. Average per capita income in the village last year was 2,900 yuan, over 70% of which came from making plaster statues.

The plaster statues used to break very easily in transit because they were made of plaster and hollow, making it hard to market them. In 1997, Hu Xinming set up the small Fengxiang Plaster Statue Plant in Liuying Village

after returning from other parts of the country working a migrant worker. Through trial and error he perfected a formula for the correct proportions of glutinous rice, cotton and pottery glue to add to the white clay to make it more resistant to breakage. This enabled these next-generation statues to be sold far and wide nationally and internationally and breathed new life

"Year of the pig" stamp issued by China Post

into Fengxiang plaster statues. There are now over 120 different types of plastic statues. In 2002 and 2003 three plaster statue works designed by Hu Xinming, "Peaceful Horse," "Rich and Powerful Lamb" and "Prosperous and Long-lived Pig," were chosen by the stamp design department of the China State Post Bureau as main pictures for its series of stamps on the 12 symbols of Chinese astrology. Hu Xinming has been called a "master of Chinese folk art" by UNESCO.

Formerly there was no mass production in the village and each individual producing household operated its own workshop. Then Hu Xinming came up with the concept of a "mass production plant with the feel of a small workshop" for the development of the Fengxiang plaster statuary industry. Hu joined together a number of producing households in the village and supplied all of them with the molds for making statues, the formula for making the plaster base and various materials required for production. The individual households were responsible for turning out a uniform line of products and Hu Xinming took responsibility for design and sales. This combination has helped the Fengxiang Plaster Statue Plant go far.

The New Appearance of the New Countryside

As the pace of urbanization increases, China's countryside falls further and further behind. In order to completely transform the countryside's lagged-behind condition, the Chinese government formulated a plan for developing a new socialist countryside. A number of towns took the lead nationwide in relying on industrialization, rural tourism and modern agriculture to improve the lot of their residents.

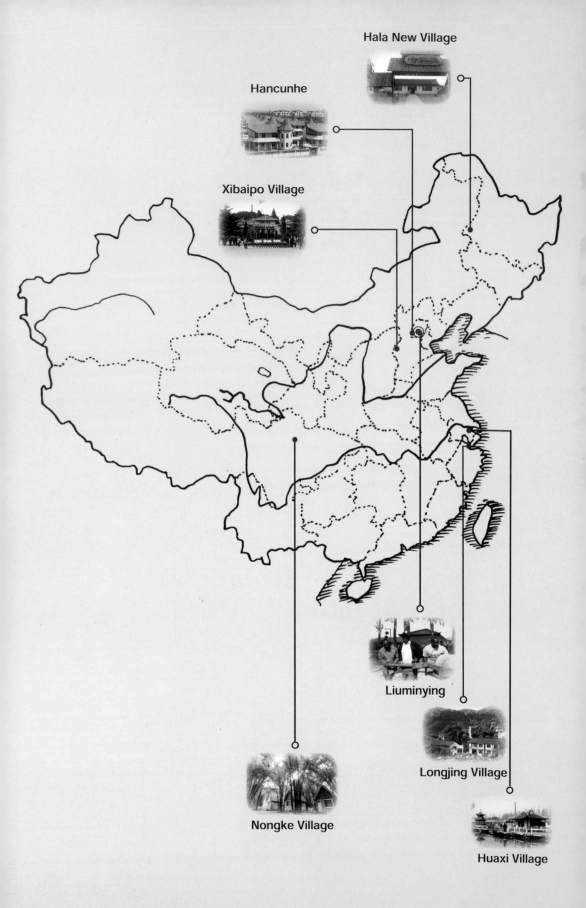

Hala New Village

Hancunhe

Xibaipo Village

Nongke Village

Liuminying

Longjing Village

Huaxi Village

Rural Tourism in Nongke Village in Pixian, Sichuan

Rural tourism is a newly developing sector in the industry that takes advantage of a combination of tourist resources, including agricultural operational activities, country life, farm scenery, country culture and living environment in the countryside, and allows interaction between the city and the countryside. It is a model for a new type of leisure activity for people looking for a healthier lifestyle and interested in getting back to nature that involves a high degree of participation. Development of rural tourism is mainly based on agriculture, the countryside and rural affairs, and gives tourists a real taste of work and life in the countryside. The tours give visitors the opportunity to eat produce that is native to the area, live in wooden houses with black tile roofs as the local residents do and enjoy themselves at a performance put on by the villagers. It is not only a one-

Wall painting of farming

time tour, but also a learning experience that will enrich the culture of tourists. The emergence of rural tourism is a part of the change in urban and rural consumer habits, a new economic growth area in the countryside, a way to absorb more surplus rural labor, and a way to increase rural incomes and helps meet the demand for recreational activities among urban residents.

Rural houses in bamboo forest

The first site for rural tourism in China is Nongke Village in Pixian, Sichuan located 18 kilometers west of Chengdu. The first household that provided rural tourism service is the Xu family estate. In 1987 all the families in Nongke Village planted flowers and grass to beautify their backyards, attracting many local visitors and visitors from outside the province. The new residence of villager Xu Jiyuan was designated at that time by the government as the reception point for visitors. This gave Yang Shoucheng, the then Party committee secretary who was a fan of the countryside, the inspiration to make the village into the "Farm Family Park." It was to be a park for visitors and a place of work for the local residents.

Recreation corridor

Beginning with the Xu family estate as the first home to accept visitors on tours of the village, Nongke Village set out on a new path of developing countryside tourism. This influenced the surrounding areas, which also began developing countryside tourism, thereby attracting large numbers of city dwellers coming to enjoy the clean pure environment of the countryside. The mushrooming sector of rural tourism began here with treks through bamboo forests, walking across stone paths, crossing small bridges, viewing the grass and trees, and enjoying country cuisine. The trees and flowers have beautified the environment and the improved environment helps boost tourism, which in turn promotes production. At the peak of its popularity in the 1990s, the rural tourism of Nongke Village included 102 households and became a prime example of countryside tourism in the Chengdu area with its motto of "eat home-cooked country food, taste the farm-fresh vegetables, stay in a country residence, experience farm work, enjoy rural pastimes and buy locally made products."

Future development plans call for the area of Nongke Village to be expanded to 10 times its original size to nearly 4,000 *mu*. Plans for the new Nongke Village include a master plan for village's makeover and a plan for distribution of production facilities and scenic sites. The 13 kilometer circular tourist route has already been widened, 8.5 kilometers of water, electricity and sewage pipelines have been laid and a 6.8-kilometer main scenic route for tourists has been fully landscaped and beautified. Nongke Village is now working hard to become a civilized and harmonious place that is a prime example of the new socialist countryside with a thriving economy, full range of functions, beautiful environment and excellent living conditions.

Enjoying leisure time to the fullest in a wide open space

Hancunhe, the Richest Village in Beijing's Suburbs

Hancunhe Village is located 40 kilometers southwest of Beijing's city center and is known as "the number one village in Beijing's suburbs." The village contains many European-style, American-style, classical-style houses, and multi-story residences, an organic food production plot with advanced technology and scientific management, the largest and best equipped office park of all Beijing's suburbs, the first locally run suburban university classroom building in Beijing and the first locally operated suburban travel agency in Beijing. Hancunhe has become a prime example of a city in the new socialist countryside.

Hancunhe was formerly known as the "uncaring river." The true picture of the poverty-stricken lives of the people was a "low-lying stinking ditch with water

Luban Park

all over the place. Clear days were marred by clouds of   Farmers' villas
dust and rain turned the area into a sea of mud. Crops
often failed and the residents were forced to eat wild
vegetables a good deal of the year. Few people had heavy
overcoats and the houses were made of mud. Every year
they looked forward to good times and constantly asked
when things would get better." In 1978 Tian Xiong, secretary of the village Party branch, with the support of
the village Party branch, took advantage of the village's
large number of mud tile workers to form the Hancunhe
Construction Brigade. After more than two decades of
hard work, the Hancunhe Construction Brigade has developed into a large state-owned construction group with
grade A assets—the Beijing Hanjian Group. Hanjian has
courageously seized opportunities and steadfastly strived
to bring honor to Beijing with the group's quality, speed,
safety, and code of conduct while battling against fierce
competition in the construction market. Tian Xiong and

Student band from
Hancunhe

his colleagues never forgot the importance of agriculture
as the foundation of the economy while they were developing the group's construction and industrial operations. The group has invested more than 10 million yuan
in agriculture over the last several years to buy nearly
100 pieces of advanced agricultural machinery to completely mechanize operations on 2,000 *mu* of farmland
from planting to harvest so that only 20 or so people are
needed for agricultural production work in normal years.
Grain production in Hancunhe has consistently exceeded
one ton per *mu* since 1992, and for four years in a row the
Fangshan District government has named Hancunhe as
a "farm with good economy of scale." Total income for
the village in 1998 was 825 million yuan, all taxes paid to
the state totaled 33.56 million yuan and the average per
capita income was 7,600 yuan. Hancunhe has been listed
as "a national model civilized town or village."

　　Development of the collective sector of the economy of

Celebration of
International Day of
Older Persons

Hancunhe has resulted in fundamental improvement in the lives of the villagers. All homes in the village have the most modern home appliances. The traditional pattern of work and life of "working from sunup to sundown" and "face to the yellow earth, back to the sky" has been completely replaced by life in a modern garden city. A total of 518 houses and 20 multi-story residential dwellings in a variety of styles have been built in the village. The poor "uncaring river" has become a city in the new socialist countryside with a full range of public facilities in which all types of businesses are booming. Residents all live in apartments and houses and people live good lives.

In addition to developing both agriculture and industry, Hancunhe has been actively expanding its tourism sector. Large numbers of tourists all over the world, visit Hancunhe to eat local home-cooked food, stay in the homes of local residents, see the new socialist countryside, and enjoy fireworks at night with the locals during the Chinese New Year celebrations.

Home to Longjing Tea—Longjing Village

Longjing Village, "the number one tea-producing village," is famous around the world because it produces large quantities of high-quality West Lake Longjing tea. West Lake Longing tea, known as the "queen of green teas," is number one among the top ten tea varieties of China. It comes in five varieties according to production locality: lion, dragon, cloud, tiger, and mulberry. West Lake Longjing tea has served as a gift and refreshment for friends for a long time, and has become a bridge of friendship in international exchange and a staple at state banquets and tea ceremonies.

Longjing tea is usually grown next to the mountains and close to water on a slope where it can receive full sunlight on clear days and the soil is acidic and drains well after rainfalls. The soil is very fertile in the area of Longjing Village, which is surrounded by mountain

Longjing Village and tea fields behind it

旭升樓

旭日重光龍獻瑞
升樓更彩井呈才

Ancient archway in the village

Performance by a gong and drum troupe to celebrate the beginning of the tea harvest

peaks and lush forests. The excellent geographical environment and quality water source provide unique natural conditions for tea production. Thanks to the mountain streams and precipitation of the area, Longjing tea has been given the honorary title of "number one tea of China" for its green color, excellent aroma, great taste and good appearance.

Longjing Village is located in the Hangzhou West Lake tourist zone bordering Xizi Lake on the east, Wuyun Mountain to the west, the eastward surging Qiantang River to the south and the cloud-scraping peaks of the north-south range of mountains to the north. The village is surrounded by fog-enshrouded mountains and resembles a green jewel embedded in the shore of Xizi Lake, a prime example of a picturesque village. The village is rich in scenic and photographic tourist attractions such as Imperial Tea Orchard, Hugong Temple and Old Dragon Well, lending a strong cultural atmosphere to this tea-growing area.

The West Lake Longjing tea-growing region is rich in cultural heritage. During the process of building a new socialist countryside, Longjing Village has adhered to a principle of "minimum interference, preservation of the original flavor and environmental concerns first,"

respected the wishes of local residents and adopted measures appropriate for local conditions and retained the original appearance wherever possible. The new Longjing Village is a concise combination of Chinese spring culture, tea culture and Buddhist culture. After renovation of the village, the beauty of the mountain streams and forests once again comprise the mountain scenery of brooks and streams in Longjing Village and the classical beauty of the buildings is an ideal place for tourists to once again see the mountain scenery and appearance of the homes of the local tea growers along the road winding up the mountain peaks alongside springs and streams.

Tea auction

The homes in Longjing Village are built along the contour of the mountain so they are at all different heights. The teahouses of the local residents have plastered walls with black tile roofs and are unique in style. The streets of the village are clean and neat and the scenery is very picturesque, drawing streams of tourists. The flat roofs were all converted to sloping black tile roofs and the doors have all been changed to baked enamel aluminum doors with wooden frames on doors and windows. The outer walls of buildings were also painted with a unified color scheme. At a high point at the entrance to the village they erected a memorial archway 7.9 meters wide and 9 meters tall with the three characters for Longjing Village written at the top. In addition, the village has erected four signs in four different languages for the convenience of tourists to explain the history, scenic spots, and public facilities of the village. These improvements have helped Longjing Village become more attractive to tourists in the West Lake scenic area.

Model of Common Prosperity—Huaxi Village

Huaxi Village in Jiangyin, Jiangsu is a model village in working for common prosperity under socialism and building a new socialist countryside. Its southern Chinese pastoral charm and rich rural life are the two main features that attract outside visitors. This beauti- ful and fertile patch of land is the cradle of Wu culture as well as the place where modern industry and commerce and the rural enterprise were born and prospered in China, leading people to call it "the number one village under heaven."

The original

Golden pagoda in Huaxi Village

area of Huaxi Village was only 0.96 square kilometers with a population of over 1,500. A small hardware plant set up in 1969 without fanfare by a villager named Wu Renbao is considered the starting point for the prosperity of the village. This poor southern village with a debt of 250,000 yuan has now become "Huaxi Village Group" covering 9 major companies and over 60 smaller enterprises with a total economic worth of over 30 billion yuan. This can only be called an economic miracle.

Huaxi Village has adhered to a path of "relying on the collective economy and working for common prosperity." Wu Renbao, the veteran Party secretary of the village, did not take a rigid and dogmatic approach to the collective economy. He forged a new approach to the development of the collective economy by taking into consideration the political climate and starting from the actual conditions of the village. Wu made the principle a "two-eight split" the way for the local residents themselves to accumulate funds and this principle is still followed today. Two tenths of the yearly bonus goes to the individual and the other eight tenths stays in the Group as stock, which pays dividends but may not be sold. During the period between June 2001 and September 2004 Huaxi Village merged with 16 nearby villages under the administrative policy of "merging townships and villages." This expanded the population to 30,000 and

Chengxiang Bridge in Huaxi Village

Most farmers in Huaxi Village live in villas.

the area to 30 square kilometers. Wu then introduced his approach in which the election of village committees and governance of the other 16 participating villages remains in the hands of the individual villages. Five other areas, economic regulation, use of cadres, arrangement of labor, welfare benefits and master plan for village development, are all unified. This approach provided for successful inclusion of these 16 villages in the common development of the new greater Huaxi Village. In 2005 Huaxi Village had a total sales volume of 30.78 billion yuan, assets of the village level collective economy totaled 11.39 billion yuan and average individual income was 65,000 yuan.

"True prosperity means having both material and intellectual prosperity." Huaxi Village has paid close attention to both economic development and ethical village governance in accordance with the law. On the basis of every family with their house and every household having their own car, the village provides the conditions for villagers to have "full pockets as well as spiritual stimulation." In the 1990s the village set up a unique "company for cultural and intellectual development" and the veteran Party secretary Wu Renbao personally wrote the "Village Song," *In Praise of Prosperity* and *Shaking off Poverty*. He also launched an education campaign throughout the greater village called "the six loves" (love for

Party, country, Huaxi Village, relatives, friends, and self), Farmers' Park which also emphasized respect for elders, thus creating an social atmosphere of respect for senior citizens and love of children. In the late 1990s Huaxi Village set up the Huaxi Special Arts Troupe, which government leaders called, "China's First Rural Troupe" and whose performances have become large banquet of cultural and intellectual treats for the people. In addition, the village put up statues representing "Eight Immortals Cross the Sea," "Summoning Zhuge Liang Three Times," "The Cowherd and the Weaver Girl" and Confucius to meet the needs of economic and social development at different times to teach the villagers through fine traditional Chinese culture. The village now has full range of facilities for cultural and recreational activities, including a public space for traditional performance artists, sport grounds, ice-skating rink, Karaoke, discos and movie theaters, providing villagers with a rich cultural life and diverse spare-time activities.

Huaxi Village has become a window for introducing people from China and abroad to China's countryside. Since the village was opened up to the outside world in 1994 nearly a million domestic and foreign tourists a year have been visiting and touring Huaxi Village and the villagers have been warmly serving them with traditional local dishes such as wonton and meat strips with chives.

Eco-Friendly Village: Liuminying

Liuminying folk custom village is located in the town of Changziying in the Daxing District of Beijing, 25 kilometers from the city center. Transportation to the village is very convenient. The village occupies a total of 146 hectares, has a total of 242 households and has a total population of 861. There are a total of 98 homes open as folk custom guesthouses, including 26 that meet municipal standards for guesthouses.

Liuminying has been depending on its excellent ecological environment, unique ecological model and culture of folk customs in recent years to create an image of the village as "the number one Chinese village in eco-agriculture," attracting the attention of the world. In particular,

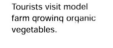

Tourists visit model farm growing organic vegetables.

Tourists from all over the world learning to make
Chinese dumplings at Liuminying Ecological
Holiday Village

Learning to use a broach grinder

UN Secretary-General Kofi Annan visiting Liuminying Ecological Farm

the village set up the folk custom tourism office, strengthened promotional efforts, standardized the management of tourist services and formulated regulations for catering to tourists, guide services and tourist safety in 2003. In addition, management of the folk custom guesthouses was unified, but operation of individual guesthouses remains independent. A regular inspection regime was set up for scenic spots and folk custom guesthouses as a free service to them. Finally, the tourism office trained guides and presenters and provided vocational training for other personnel in the local tourist industry, organized outside visits and study for people operating guesthouses, provides training classes to improve service skills, issues business licenses for guesthouses and publish news about eco-agriculture and folk tourism and plans for all activities online.

Liuminying has been listed in the "the top 500 in global environmental protection" by the UN Environment Program. Liuminying, the number one Chinese village in eco-agriculture, has been developing eco-agricultural demonstration sites for two decades, attracting tourists from 138 countries and regions of the world. Liuminying has been gradually developed into a hi-tech holiday village for folk custom tourism that combines eco-tourism and folk custom tourism as the main feature, complimented by food and beverage, entertainment and exercise venues, with intensive cultivation, aquaculture, harvesting, fishing, barbeque, lodging and agricultural sightseeing. The Liumingying tourist area consists of four zones, two parks and two centers. The four zones are the hi-tech organic agricultural demonstration plot, contaminant-free organic vegetable demonstration plot, folk custom tourist zone and demonstration zone for comprehensive use of methane and solar power; the two parks are the ecological park and agricultural park; and the two centers are the international ecological agricultural academic, study and training center and restaurant, conference and entertainment center.

The State Environmental Protection Administration named Liuminying as an organic agriculture demonstration base in 2000. Liuminying has also been named as a "national advanced organization in building spiritual civilization," one of the "top 1,000 villages in the country in planting forests and landscaping," "national agricultural tourism demonstration site," "Beijing patriotic education base" and "Beijing folk custom tourism village" It has been recognized by the State Environmental Protection Administration as an "organic farm."

Xibaipo Red Tourism

Xibaipo is located in Pingshan County, Hebei Province. It was once the location of the CPC Central Committee and the headquarters of the PLA and is now one of the most famous destinations in the country on the Red Tourism.

Xibaipo is a small mountain village on the north bank of the Hutuo River in the mountains in western Hebei. The scenery is beautiful and the soil is fertile here. The village is located in the center of Pingshan County nestled between the North China Plains and Taihang Mountain. Xibaipo was selected to be the command center for the liberation of the entire country and planning for the establishment of New China. It enjoys unique geographical conditions and natural environment plus a revolutionary base and political strength built up over many years. It is

Xibaipo Memorial
Museum

surrounded by mountains on three sides and by water on the fourth. To the west is Taihang Mountain, to the east is the Central Hebei Plains and only 90 kilometers away is the important city of Shijiazhuang. It is an easy place to get to, easy to defend and hard to attack, a good mountain retreat in times of crisis and a good base from which to attack the city when the time was right. The fairly well developed rural economy of the area ensured adequate economic support for both the army and the people and provided the material base for locating the Central Committee there.

Site of the Second Plenary Session of the Seventh Central Committee of the Chinese Communist Party

The Central Committee was only located in Xibaipo for 10 months, but this period was a brilliant chapter in the annals of the Chinese revolution. For this reason, along with Jinggang Mountain, Ruijin and Yan'an, it is considered one the birthplaces of the revolution. The time the Central Committee was located in the village marked a turn in the great history of the Chinese revolution as

Former residence of Zhu De

well as the most successful time in the course of the communist democratic revolution. The new-democratic revolution led by the Central Committee gained nationwide victory during this time, opening the way for the Party to switch the focus of their efforts from the countryside to the cities and from warfare to development, and to begin the change from new democracy to socialism.

Ground was broken for the Xibaipo Memorial Museum in 1976 to cover a total area of 13,400 square meters with a floor space of 3,344 square meters. The museum is built is the form of a two-story step-style courtyard dwelling and a corridor runs around all four sides of the courtyard. The museum's exhibits are combined with the latest audio-visual equipment to show Xibaipo's position in history and far-reaching influence in a concise way. The museum is divided into four educational areas or sightseeing sites, Former Site of the Central Committee, Exhibit of Relics, Park of Calligraphy and Carvings, and

Elderly man sells calabashes and other local products.

Traditional Education Project. The Former Site of the Central Committee contains the residences of Mao Zedong, Liu Shaoqi, Zhou Enlai and Ren Bishi and the site of the headquarters of the PLA. Between the front and back courtyards is the site of the Second Plenary Session of the Seventh Central Committee. In the westernmost part of the courtyard is the site of the September 1948 meeting of the Central Committee.

As everyone knows, "old revolutionary base area" is almost synonymous with "lagged-behind area," and Xibaipo also went through such a period in its history. In recent years, however, the people of Xibaipo have been making increasingly steady and sound progress in restructuring local agriculture and improving their lives, relying on the area's excellent geographical conditions and unique political strength and strong efforts to develop pastoral tourism and red tourism. All 67 households in the village have built new houses and greatly improved their living conditions. There are now 64 bed and breakfast inns and tourist hotels operating in the village involving 95% of the village residents. There are 23 bed and breakfast inns that can handle a total of 400 guests and 15 home-cooked country cuisine restaurants that can handle 500 diners at a time. Everyone in the village, with the exception of a few senior citizens and children in school, is involved in the tourist and service trades. Including people from outside the area, there are over 200 people involved in providing in-home tourist services with an average yearly income of 4,711 yuan. "Every household has a project, everybody has a job" is a vivid description of Xibaipo today. The residents of Xibaipo collectively set up a pollution-free vegetable production plot covering 18 *mu* in order to accelerate the development of pastoral tourism. This plot produces a total income of 180,000 yuan and more per year. The total income from tourism and services in all of Xibaipo in 2005 topped 1.3 million yuan.

Today's Xibaipo, with its crisscrossing streams, rows of poplar trees and beautiful environment attracts hordes of visitors to the village.

Tahur Hala New Village

Tahur means "the original place," in other words, hometown. The Tahur ethnic group is originally from the Zeja River area north of Heilongjiang, but military invasion from the Russian Czar in the early 17th century forced them to move southward. When they came to the Nenjiang River area east of Greater Hinggan Mountains and saw how beautiful the natural environment was, they decided to settle there.

During the centuries the Tahur have lived in the Nenjiang River area, their long-time hunting and fishing lifestyle have made them into an agile and brave people

Totem of the Tahur ethnic group, made from hawks and hockey balls beaten together

and led them to create many sports activities closely tied to their work and lives. From ancient times, they have played a game very similar to field hockey, which the Tahur called "Beikuo." In 1976 China organized its first professional hockey team around some young Tahur men. These young men from the remote countryside were selected through fierce competition and catapulted into the international arena thanks to their skill in Beikuo handed down to them from their ancestors.

Located in Hala Village, Ya'ersai Town in the Meilisi District of Qiqihar is a Tahur village with a long history. In the past, the villagers toiled from sunrise to sunset on an average of 2.5 *mu* per person, always hoping for better

Typical yard of Tahur farmers

times, but always reaping poverty. In 1998 a major flood on the Nenjiang River destroyed their fields and changed their reluctance to abandon their reliance on agriculture.

With the financial assistance of the National Committee of the Chinese People's Political Consultative Conference and the National Charity Association of China, the next year they rebuilt the village into a modern new village, giving the villagers a beautiful new home. The village was divided into four residential areas with a common style in a natural distribution. Of the 300 households in the village, 182 are Tahur households. The total population is 1,036, of which 70% are Tahur. This is the new Tahur village with a pronounced Tahur character.

In order to solve the problem of unsanitary and unsightly conditions caused by raising cattle and sheep, in the fall of 2001, the village built two high-standard cattle barns with 1,500 square meters of floor space to centralize all livestock breeding in the village. Then in 2002, the village built a plant to turn large quantities of straw

Uninhibited Tahur dance

waste into gas, which also solved the problem of piles of straw chaff littering the environment. The villagers organized an ethnic dance troupe especially to promote ethnic culture. The troupe often performs in the village and is sometimes invited to perform outside the area, and their performances are loved by villagers and tourists alike.

As part of the process of building a modern new village and improving infrastructure, the village has carried out projects to build a loop road around the village, improve water and electricity supply, install an automatic telephone exchange, and beautify the natural environment. In addition, the village now has a local clinic, primary school, department store, hotel, parking garage, cultural and sports center, low-pollution food exhibition hall and retirement home. In 2002 the village

Tahur woman serving drinks to a guest

built a Tahur theme park with a hotel styled after a Tahur residence and food and beverage service center featuring ethnic cuisine, which also has entertainment venues such as children's play center, open-air horse track and large fishing pond. The new park has attracted large numbers of visitors who come to appreciate the beauty of nature and learn about Tahur ethnic customs.

Hala New Village is now taking great strides to improve its ecological environment and strengthen its ethnic character. People work hard to make the village more modern and sophisticated and improve conditions for tourism.